Carlucco and the Queen of Hearts

The Blasphemer

George Rosie

Chapman Publications

Published by
Chapman
4 Broughton Place
Edinburgh EH1 3RX
Scotland

The publisher acknowledges the financial assistance of the
Scottish Arts Council in the publication of this volume.

A catalogue record for this volume is
available from the British Library.

ISBN 0-906772-43-5

Cover design by Fred Crayk
Typeset by Peter Cudmore
Photographs from the original stage productions by David Liddle

Printed by
Mayfair Printers
Print House
William Street
Sunderland
Tyne and Wear

Contents

Foreword

Considering the rich seam of drama that runs through Scotland's history, it is striking how poorly it has been exploited in the past by Scottish playwrights. Its dramatis personae – Macbeth, Mary Stuart, Lucia di Lammermoor – have given us the essence of tragedy, but they have been brought to life by writers from other nations. There are of course epics of the stage like Sir David Lindsay's Ane Satyre of the Thrie Estaitis; there were some 19th century plays based on the novels of Sir Walter Scott; James Bridie flirted with Scottish history; more recently John McGrath has tackled it head-on, while others, like Liz Lochhead, have made fun of it; the use of social realism in conveying aspects of Scottish rural and urban life has made for some vigorous theatre in the last decade or so, though it would be stretching a point to classify that as historical drama. But there has been a distinct and definite reluctance to exploit the cast-list of Scotland's Kings and Queens, the tales of jealousy and betrayal at court, the scheming prelates and warring nobles, the bloody battles won and lost, and though these have been the inspiration for great Scottish literature, whether in the form of novels, poetry or song, few native playwrights have chosen to grapple with them.

This may be partly because, in marked contrast to the richness of its literary past, Scotland can only boast what Edwin Morgan has described as a "thin and broken dramatic tradition". Up until the 20th century, there have been few Scottish playwrights of note, and nothing by way of indigenous theatre to compare with the richness of English drama from the 16th century onwards. With little royal patronage, and faced by a disapproving Kirk, the theatre failed to flourish in Scotland, and there is no body of memorable work for the stage between the 17th and 19th centuries. The play *Douglas*, which excited a first-night enthusiast to cry "Whaur's yer Wullie Shakespeare noo?" may have seemed a great theatrical event to its mid-18th century audiences, but it can scarcely be said to have stood the test of time. Playwrights, managers, even actors and actresses tended to be exports from the south, and English repertory dominated the stage. It was not until 1909 that a Scottish company, the Glasgow Repertory Theatre, set out as its aim "the encouragement and development of purely Scottish drama by providing a stage and acting company which will be peculiarly adapted for the production of plays national in character, written by Scottish men and women of letters." Since then, there has been great enthusiasm for Scottish theatre, though there is still no National Theatre of Scotland.

George Rosie's plays *Carlucco and the Queen of Hearts* and *The Blasphemer*, published for the first time here, meet head-on the challenges of scale and of language that may help explain why the dramatic tradition in Scots literature is not stronger. The great events and characters of history can be daunting, and not every playwright has the courage of a Shakespeare in bringing the clash of battle or the death of kings onto the narrow confines of a stage. Equally, to achieve authenticity of dialect while remaining understandable to a 20th century English-speaking audience is no mean feat. Rosie, a journalist who has always been fascinated by the history of his own country, has neither shrunk from large themes, nor hesitated to meet the challenge of conveying the conversational Scots of 200 years ago to a modern audience. There is nothing here to baffle even the most English of theatre-goers, but at the same time the way in which the language of the 17th and 18th century is conveyed carries complete conviction.

In *The Blasphemer* Rosie takes as his backdrop the religious conflicts of the 17th century, and in describing the trial and execution of the student Thomas Aikenhead, the last man hanged for blasphemy in Scotland, he shows freedom of expression in fatal conflict with the political determinism of the times. He approaches the story through the tortured memories of the Edinburgh minister George Meldrum, who, by reporting Aikenhead's irreverent views on Deism and Christianity to the authorities, effectively sent him to the gallows. In Meldrum we catch a whiff of that stern Presbyterianism that drove the Covenanters to half a century of rebellion, in a man who cannot grapple with the cheerful nonconformity of a youthful mind. His remorse on realising that, by informing on Aikenhead, he has condemned him to death, makes him a real if pathetic figure, a tool in the hands of scheming politicians. It is the designs of Lord Chancellor Polwarth and Sir James Stewart of Goodtrees which ensure that Aikenhead is hanged, and through them we gain an insight into the complexities of that dangerous time when Scotland swung between Jacobitism and the Whigs. Rosie's achievement is to succeed in crystallising the debate without interfering with what is essentially a human drama.

Carlucco and the Queen of Hearts also has a victim as its principal character – in this case that most unsatisfactory of Scottish heroes, Charles Edward Stuart. Not the romantic leader of Prestonpans or even Culloden, but the wreck of a man in later life, still pretender to the English throne, eking out his exiled days in Florence, an embarrassment to the governments of two countries. Although it may sometimes appear that Bonnie Prince Charlie's career ended on the day he sailed for France aboard the frigate *L'Heureux*, he lived longer in exile than he had as a young contender for the throne. Again Rosie is fascinated by political manipulation, the individual at the mercy of conflicting powers. He approaches his theme through the eyes of Sir Horace Mann, the British government's envoy in Florence, whose reports kept the Hanoverian throne in close touch with events in Italy; in particular with the marital prospects of Charles Edward and his new wife, Louise de Stolberg – the "Queen of Hearts". The question of whether they might yet produce a legitimate heir to lay claim to the English throne was a real one despite the crumbling of the young pretender's own prospects. This is a portrait of power in decline, of a man whose life has crashed from great expectations to abject failure, yet who retains shreds of royal dignity even as he is subjected by his enemies and his wife to political and sexual humiliation.

George Rosie has a journalist's eye for a good story; as a historian he has ensured the authenticity of time, place and language needed to bring them alive. But it is as a playwright that he has made an important addition to Scottish literature. In doing so he has gone some way to correcting an imbalance that stretches back over many years, and has deprived us for too long of the vigorous drama that Scotland's history can yield. Rosie demonstrates that, if the craftsman can be found, there is no lack of raw material waiting to be worked on.

Magnus Linklater

Carlucco and the Queen of Hearts

First performed by

Fifth Estate

at the

Netherbow Theatre, Edinburgh

7 August 1991

Charles Edward Stuart .... Robert Carr

Louise de Stolberg .... Eilidh Fraser

Count Vittorio Alfieri .... Alexander West

Sir Horace Mann.. Robin Thomson

Catherine de Maltzam... Ashley Jensen

Jonathan Rudd .... Steven McNicoll

John Stewart .... Allan Sharpe

Stage Manager .... Estelle van Warmelo

Deputy Stage Manager .... Jo Webster

Assistant Stage Manager .... Owen Baldock

Director.. Sandy Neilson

Designer... Paul Ambrose Wright

Lighting Design .... John Cassidy

Costume Design.. Hania Dzikowska

Scenic Artist .... Mike McLoughlin

Production Manager .... Sean Miller

Carlucco and the Queen of Hearts
Dramatis Personae

Charles Edward Stuart: A man in his late fifties; tall, stooping, overweight and running to seed. His complexion is raddled with drink, flushed and reddened. His formerly superb physique is in a state of collapse. He has scurvy sores on his legs (a legacy of his 'flight across the heather') which cannot be healed, and cause him constant pain. He drinks constantly. By the end of his marriage to Louise de Stolberg he is consuming anything between six and eight bottle of fortified Cyprus wine a day. His guts and liver are ruined; he suffers from flatulence, and from constant pains in his belly. He is also prone to dizzy spells and fainting fits.

For all that, he is an impressive figure. There is a kind of collapsed nobility about him. There is dignity and ability in the ruins. He is often addled and wandering, but is capable of flashes of insight, wit, and shrewdness. He is suspicious and he is, in most respects, no fool. And he *always* wears the blue ribbon and badge of the Order of the Garter, a remnant of British royalty that he hung onto. There is a kind of heroic pathos about him. At the same time he is inclined to blame others for his failure. Nothing is ever his own fault, or his own responsibility.

Louise de Stolberg: Louise was aged 20 when she married Charles in 1782. By the time of the events in Florence she is a young woman in her late 20s. She is blond, handsome rather than pretty, and very bright. Although quite bookish, she is outgoing and sociable. In fact she is a fairly determined socialiser. She has a good singing voice and likes to strum on a lute and guitar. She is described as being a blue stocking *manque*, with a fondness for intellectual and literary men. Although she is no intellectual herself, she is clever, determined, wheedling and very manipulative. She is flirtatious, a good talker, quite well read, and very sexy.

Some writers have sympathised with her for being trapped in a gruesome marriage, a young woman thirled to a rapidly ageing, and increasingly brutal man. Others have characterised her as an ambitious, stone-hearted little schemer whose treatment of Charles hastened his downfall. This seems the more likely interpretation of her character. She was certainly a resourceful adulteress, and had a string of affairs under the Pretender's nose – Alfieri was only the last of them.

Catherine de Maltzam: She was Louise's 'lady-in-waiting'. Little has been written about her except that she was a Swabian (ie German) lady who was about ten years older than Louise. She is described – vaguely – as being pretty, slightly overweight, and rather untidy. She dotes on her mistress and is involved in all her little stratagems – she is certainly heavily involved in the final 'escape' to the convent. Possiby she is in love with Louise, although she did dally with the travelling companion of one of Louise's admirers, the Swiss *litterateur* Bonstetten. She talks with a (south) German accent.

Vittorio Alfieri: A man of Louise's age, or slightly older. A well-heeled nobleman from the Piedmont, Alfieri is a subject of the King of Sardinia, and something of a Byronic figure (decades before Byron invented the idea of the Romantic poet). He is described as gung-ho and reckless, and ready to commit everything to the throw of a dice. Tall, red-headed, good-looking, intense, he seems to be an enthusiastic womaniser.

He is also a fanatical horseman, and never travels anywhere without a stable of four or five thoroughbreds. He is widely travelled (for an Italian), having visited Russia, Germany, Scandinavia, England, and Spain and Portugal. For all his philandering ways, Alfieri seems to be genuinely devoted to Louise. After she escaped from the clutches of Charles, the couple lived together quite happily until he died in 1805.

Sir Horace Mann: An intriguing figure. Mann was the British Government's 'envoy' in Florence for almost fifty years. After settling in the city he never once returned to England. Nicknamed 'Mini' Mann, he is waspish, foppish, and camp as a row of tents. There is a general agreement that Mann is a homosexual. Certainly he is unmarried, and most writers talk of his 'mincing' manners and fondness for the 'travelling boys' of England (ie the young aristocrats on the Grand Tour). At the time of the play he is in his late sixties.

For all his elaborate manners and dainty *mores*, Mann is a fiercely loyal Hanoverian, and never hesitates to 'bully and browbeat' the Popes in the Hanoverian interest. Mann's effusive, intimate letters to his 'dearest friend' Horace Walpole are remarkable documents of life and politics in 18th century Florence (and Rome). Mann is instrumental in making sure that the Vatican refuses to acknowledge Charles as King of England when his father James ('The Old Pretender') dies in 1766. He is a ruthless and determined British diplomat: King George had no more effective functionary than Horace Mann.

Jonathan Rudd: Mann's secretary. A fictional character. In his early middle years, a soberly dressed, stockily built Englishman, possibly with a Yorkshire accent. Like his master, Rudd is a zealous Hanoverian who despises the Stuarts, Catholics and most foreigners.

John Stewart A middle-aged Gael from Atholl who had been with Charles Stuart since before the Jacobite insurrection. A loyal member of the Stuart household.

Act I

Scene One

Sir Horace Mann's house at the Casa Manetti by the Ponte de Trinità, Florence. The house is set on the Arno; near enough, it was said, to catch fish from the windows. Sir Horace Mann is the British envoy in Tuscany. He is a tall, spare, overdressed man in his late sixties. He wears an old-fashioned heavy wig, and richly brocaded clothes. His face is powdered and made up.

Also present is Mann's clerk, Jonathan Rudd. Rudd is in his early forties, dressed in a sober business suit of brown or grey. He wears his hair in a club, tied back with a black bow. Rudd is a Yorkshireman; blunt, efficient, hard-working. He is a loyal Hanoverian apparatchik.

The two men play to one another's personalities. In the face of Mann's florid mannerisms and camp gestures, Rudd is exaggeratedly – maybe even perversely – blunt and down-to-earth. Rudd's crudeness inspires Mann to greater flights of campery. But Mann is always the boss.

Mann: Whispers in the gallery, Rudd. I hear whispers in the gallery. Every box at the theatre is buzzing with rumour.

Rudd: Sir Horace?

Mann: The Queen of Hearts, Rudd. The Queen of Hearts. They tell me there's a new suitor at her court. A young man panting for her favours. Do we know about him?

Rudd shuffles his papers and extracts one from the pile. He reads in a harsh, flat, heavily accented voice.

Rudd: Count Vittorio Alfieri. Poet and tragedian.

Mann: (*laughing*) Oh dear! Another scribbler. Her Ladyship does have a taste for the *literati* does she not? Is he Tuscan, this 'poet and tragedian'?

Rudd: Piedmontese.

Mann: I didn't know they *had* poets in Piedmont.

Rudd: There are poets everywhere.

Mann: Alas! I fear that you're right. And what do we know about him?

Rudd: (*consulting his paper*) Rich family. In fact a very rich family. Father died when he was a child. Well educated. Age 28, or thereabouts. Well travelled. France, England, Germany, Denmark, Spain, Portugal, even Russia. Fond of ladies and horses.

Mann: Both of which he rides with equal skill, I suppose.

Rudd: So they say.

Mann: Political?

Rudd: Only in a *poetical* kind of way.

Mann: (*archly*) Handsome?

Rudd: The ladies seem to think so. Big fellow. Bit of a brawler I'd say. Supposed to have a short fuse. Ill-natured bugger is my guess.

Mann: (*sardonically*) Surely you mean a highly bred young man of fine temper.

Rudd: If you say so, Sir Horace.

Mann: And does this Count, ah ...

Rudd: Alfieri.

Mann: Does Count Alfieri's literary production amount to much? Does the Queen of Hearts have a new Dante Alighieri swooning at her feet?

Rudd: (*with a shrug*) I've no idea. He's written some sort of verse drama called Cleopatra. A few poems. Sonnets. That sort of thing.

Mann: Never much of a man for the theatre, were you Rudd?

Rudd: No, Sir.

Mann: Oh well! And does *Mister* Stuart know anything of this, *liaison*?

Rudd: (*shrugging*) The two gentlemen have yet to be introduced. Or so I'm told.

Mann: So where does the Queen of Hearts *receive* this new champion from the Lists of Literature?

Rudd: They meet by chance.

Mann: Of course they do. Where?

Rudd: In gardens. On the street. Beside the Arno. In the Cathedral. In Vasari's corridor. Outside the Pitti Palace.

Mann: Very decorous.

Rudd: They're both *very* fond of the Uffizi.

Mann: A very dangerous place, I always think. All that *beautifully* painted flesh. One can almost see it quiver. Signor Titian's 'Venus of Urbino' alone is enough to, well, *agitate* the passions of the most decorous of art lovers.

Rudd: Is that the picture of the fat wench lying in the buff scratching her twat?

Mann: (*with mock horror*) Rudd, please. She is *not* scratching her, ah, whatever it was you said. She is modestly covering her nakedness with her hand.

Rudd: (*grinning*) Well whatever she's doing, she looks like she's enjoying herself.

Mann: Oh dear. I can see that the Renaissance has still to reach Yorkshire. And do we know who introduced these two art-loving young people?

Rudd: There's a story about that. They say that Alfieri first came across her in the Uffizi. She was admiring that portrait of that mad bastard, what's his name, Charles the Twelfth of Sweden. Who's some kind of Royal ancestor of hers. Is that right?

Mann: So she believes.

Rudd: Anyway. This Alfieri was so struck by the Stolberg charms...

Mann: Which are undoubted.

Rudd: ... That he ordered himself a suit of clothes *exactly* like the one worn by King Charles in the portrait.

Mann: How dashing.

Rudd: Then the fool paraded up and down outside her window outside the Palazzo Guadagni. On the off-chance that she'd notice him. Daft bugger.

Mann: (*laughing*) What a good story. I don't believe a word of it, of course. But it'll give the Florentines something else to giggle about.

Rudd: (*dourly*) Do they *need* something else to giggle about?

Mann: Don't be such a kill-joy. And besides, it does make the young man and his *amorata* look rather silly. And now. To the serious question.

Rudd: Is he fucking her?

Mann: (*sardonically*) I do wish you wouldn't beat about the bush, Rudd. It's so annoying. Well, is he?

Rudd: Not yet. But he will.

Mann: (*thoughtfully*) Mmm. That bothers me. Strapping lad like that.

Rudd: Why? The Stuart princess, darling of the Jacobites, being debauched under the nose of the Pretender? Sounds perfect.

Mann: Oh that part's *very* acceptable. But what His Britannic Majesty might *not* find acceptable is a little Alfieri being passed off as a little Stuart.

Rudd: Ah.

Mann: Some tiny olive-skinned Jacobite with a talent for poetry emerging to lead the cause. For another generation.

Rudd: Aye. There is that.

Mann: It needs watching, Rudd. Careful watching. Is our, ah, friend at the Stuart court still being paid?

Rudd: Aye.

Mann: That's good. Then make sure we keep a very close eye on the Queen of Hearts' laundry basket.

Rudd: Her laundry basket?

Mann: I want every rag she wears examined every day. Every rag. Bed linen too. Is that understood?

Rudd: Understood.

Mann: If the Queen of Hearts stops bleeding, then I want to be the first to know. After the lady herself, of course.

Rudd: You will be.

Mann: (*with a trace of menace*) I do hope so, Rudd. I do hope so. Charles Stuart may be a rag doll of a man. But rag dolls can be useful puppets. And made to dance to a tune that King George would never whistle.

Scene Two

*The Palazzo Guadagni, Florence, home of the Stuart court in exile.
Louise de Stolberg is seated in a comfortable chair, doing something
respectable; embroidery, perhaps, or reading a volume of improving
literature.*

> *Catherine de Maltzam, her lady-in-waiting is sitting across from
> her. Louise leans towards her conspiratorially.*

Louise: Now remember Catherine. You're in love with him. You're besotted.
You have eyes only for him. His every utterance is a pearl of wisdom.

Catherine: But Madam, are you sure ...

Louise: Listen to me. He's your hero. He is Daphnis to your Chloë.

Catherine: Madam. A man like Count Alfieri would never... I cannot do
such a thing...

Louise: (*sharply*) Of course you can. You must.

Catherine: I'm too *old*.

Louise: Rubbish, Catherine. You're not yet forty. He's nearly thirty. That's no
difference at all. Many men *prefer* older women such as yourself.

Catherine: (*half amused, half convinced*) But milady ...

Louise: (*sharply*) Catherine! You've got to do this for me.

Catherine: (*reluctantly*) I'll try.

Louise: (*sternly*) No. You must do *more* than try. You must *do it*.

Catherine: I... Oh, very well.

Louise: (*giggling*) It's very simple. All you want in this world is for Count
Alfieri to throw you down on the floor and ravish you to within an inch of
your life. Now is that such a bad thought?

Catherine: (*giggling*) Madam! Please!

Louise: No, seriously. It's important that His Majesty believes that the Count
comes here to see you. We *must* make him believe that.

Catherine: I understand. But what shall I do?

Louise: Oh for God's sake. Nothing that I haven't seen you do a dozen times
before. Flirt a little. Make cow eyes at him. Show some bosom. Flaunt
your backside. It's all in the cause of love.

Catherine: Love?

Louise: *My* love.

Catherine: (*resentfully*) Yes, milady.

Louise: And don't take on like that! A lady of your years should be grateful
for the attentions of such a handsome man. Even if they are counterfeit.

Catherine: (*with a trace of bitterness*) Yes, my lady.

> *John Stewart enters. He is a soberly dressed, middle aged man. Very
> much the senior household servant. he has been with the Stuart
> household for many years.*

Louise: Yes, Stewart?

Stewart: A Count Vittorio Alfieri, your Highness.

Louise: Oh yes. Thank you Stewart. Please show Count Alfieri in. (*to Catherine*) Remember now. You are Psyche to his Cupid. Ready to throw yourself at his feet.

> *The women giggle. Alfieri is ushered in. He is a tall, well-set-up man. His style is Byronic, dramatic. He crosses to Louise. She offers her hand to be kissed. He bows low over it.*

Alfieri: Your Majesty. I am honoured.

Louise: Count Alfieri. You've met my lady-in-waiting – and my friend – Mademoiselle Catherine de Maltzam...

> *Alfieri bows to Catherine and kisses her hand, rather less enthusiastically,*

Alfieri: Mademoiselle de Maltzam.

> *Catherine holds on to his hand rather longer than she should.*

Catherine: Count Vittorio. I've been looking forward to your visit. It is good to see you again.

> *She glances nervously at Louise who smiles. Alfieri is slightly startled by the warmth of Catherine's welcome. He stares at her.*

Alfieri: Ah... thank you, Mademoiselle.

Louise: Please be seated, Count Alfieri.

> *Alfieri goes to sit on a large, high-backed gilt chair.*

Louise: (*hastily*) No, not there. That's His Majesty's special chair. That's very Royal.

Alfieri: Ah. Forgive me.

Catherine: Come and sit by me, Sir.

Alfieri: That will be a pleasure, Mademoiselle.

Louise: His Majesty will be with us shortly.

Alfieri: Ah...

Louise: Affairs of state, you know. Matters of great moment. His time is not his own. Not like that of lesser mortals such as we.

Alfieri: I'm looking forward to meeting your Royal husband.

Louise: Then I trust you won't be disappointed.

> *The two women laugh. Alfieri looks from one to the other with some unease.*

Alfieri: I'm sure I won't be. Kings are a rare breed. Especially Kings of England.

Louise: Do you think so? England seems to have twice as many kings as most countries. One in England and one here in Florence.

Alfieri: Counterfeit in the place of gold, Madam. An arrangement still to be corrected by the hand of history. Alas!

Louise: But would you believe that there are still those who ask – which is which?

> *There is the sound of coughing and wheezing. A belch and a fart. Catherine giggles. Louise smiles. Alfieri looks startled.*

Louise: (*caustically*) Ah. The chink of gold itself, I believe.

Louise leans over to Alfieri with sudden intimacy in her voice.

Louise: Remember Vittorio, he's *Royalty.* At all times. He insists on it. And don't be surprised by the *smell*...

Alfieri nods.

> *Charles Edward Stuart, Pretender to the throne of Britain and Ireland, shuffles into the room. What has been a magnificent physique is now in decay. He stoops. One of his legs is bandaged. He is plainly just out of his sleep. He mutters to himself. His wig is askew. He wears the blue ribbon of the garter slung across his left shoulder.*
>
> *Alfieri stands when Charles moves into the room.*

Louise: Your Majesty, may I present to you, Count Vittorio Alfieri.

> *Charles slumps into a large gilt chair, nods and extends his right hand to be kissed. Alfieri drops to one knee and does the needful.*

Alfieri: Your Majesty. It is an honour to meet you.

Charles: Not at all Count...

Alfieri: Alfieri, Sir. Vittorio Alfieri.

Charles: Ah yes. Count Alfieri. You'll have to forgive me. I've been reading and scribbling all day. My eyes are about to drop out, and my fingers feel like sticks of kindling.

Louise: My poor husband.

Charles: A man has his duty.

> *Charles rings a bell at his table. A few moments later John Stewart appears with a tray bearing a bottle of wine and a single glass. He pours Charles a large measure, which he downs instantly. Stewart pours another, then Charles waves him away.*

Charles: Alfieri, Alfieri. You're one of Her Majesty's *literary* friends, am I right? The one from the Piedmont. A subject of the King of Sardinia.

Alfieri: (*slightly surprised*) Yes, Sire. That's right.

Charles: My wife tells me you're some kind of poet.

Alfieri: Of the humbler sort.

Charles: That's good. I like poets.

Louise: Count Alfieri's poetry has many admirers, Your Majesty. One of whom (*she glances at Catherine*) is not far from this chair.

> *Catherine obliges with a simper. Alfieri looks shifty. Charles catches the glance and smiles benevolently.*

Charles: An admirer at court, eh, Count Alfieri? No bad thing for a poet with ambitions.

Alfieri: (*puzzled*) Yes, Sire. I'm sure you're right.

Charles: Wrote a poem myself once. For our wedding day, as I recall. Damned if I can remember how it goes. Do you remember, Louise?

Louise: Of course. How could I forget.

Charles: (*after a pause*) Well then...?

Louise: (*reciting*) 'This crown is due to you by me
              And none shall love you more than me'.
Charles: That's the one. 'This crown is due to you by me. And none shall love
    you more than me.' What do you think, Alfieri?
Alfieri: (*politely*) Charming, Sire. Memorable.
Charles: (*laughing*) It's rubbish, Alfieri. The merest doggerel. But its good of
    you not to be rude.

    Alfieri realises that the Stuart is an easy man to underestimate.
    Louise tries to recover the situation.

Louise: Count Alfieri is engaged in writing several historical tragedies.
Charles: Several, eh? Well my advice is do 'em one at a time. Never
    overstretch yourself. The consequences can be dire.
Louise: On such matters, the King knows whereof he speaks.
Charles: I do, Madam, I do indeed.
Alfieri: It's sound advice, Sir. I'm sure.
Charles: Which you'll doubtless ignore. Well, well. Young men must have
    their heads. I had mine.
Louise: As the world knows. With admiration.

    He looks at her and grunts.

Charles: Forgive me, Alfieri, would you care for some wine?
Alfieri: Thank you, Sir, but no.
Charles: Are you sure? It's the best Cyprus wine that money can buy. The
    smell of the coast of Africa in every glass. Not that I've ever smelled the
    coast of Africa.
Alfieri: No thank you, Sire. I've dined.
Charles: Not some kind of abstainer, are you?
Alfieri: Nothing like that. Just a man with a full belly.
Charles: And a healthy one, by the look of you. I had a healthy belly once.
    And a pair of good strong legs. Once. Now look at me. Guts ruined. There
    are days I can hardly breathe. And sores in my legs that create the pains of
    hell itself.

    He shifts awkwardly in his seat with a faint groan.

Charles: And problems in certain places too indelicate to mention.
Louise: Your Majesty's health is improving every day. You'll soon be the,
    what is it, the 'Bonnie Prince' that the people of Scotland worshipped.
Charles: Some of the people.
Louise: Then shame on those who didn't.
Charles: *Che serà, serà.* Ever been to Scotland, Alfieri?
Alfieri: No Sir. But I have travelled in England.
Charles: (*eagerly*) Have you now? D'ye know London?
Alfieri: Yes I do.
Charles: Ah, my own Capital. My God how I do envy you, Sir.
Alfieri: Envy?
Charles: Aye, Sir, envy. To come and go as you please. To travel. To visit
    London whenever the mood is on you. Such freedom.

Alfieri: I see.
Charles: And do you enjoy my capital?
Alfieri: I do, Sire. Very much.
Charles: Why?
Alfieri: (*with an Italianate shrug*) What shall I say? Handsome buildings. Clean streets. Good theatres. Pleasant parks. Hardly a beggar to be seen. A clean, well-dressed and industrious people.
Charles: The finest people on earth, the English.
Louise: And thriving, it seems, under King George.
Charles: (*irritated*) Thriving under Protestantism, perhaps. A land without *Popes* has many advantages.
Alfieri: (*smoothly*) And how much more would England thrive under its God-given monarch?
Charles: You might think so, Count Alfieri. But there are limits to what Monarchs can achieve.
Louise: Especially here in Florence.
Charles: Your meaning, Madam?
Louise: (*smoothly*) I was thinking how *hard* the Grand Duke has been working to create a new agriculture, a new trade, a new polity in Tuscany. And how little success he's had. Poor man. Life must be so *difficult* for him.
Charles: (*sourly*) If the Grand Duke of Tuscany acknowledged his friends, the Lord might favour him rather more.
Louise: But tell us more of England, Count Alfieri. Did you visit other parts? Outside of London?
Alfieri: I did, Madam. I saw the naval town of Portsmouth. I visited Salisbury. I went to Bath – a handsome little city. Then to Bristol. Oh, and the colleges of Oxford.
Charles: Then you've seen more of England than England's King.
Alfieri: It grieves me to think so, Sire.
Charles: The truth is, Alfieri. Apart from one little *sub rosa* outing to London – where I spent my days skulking in corners – all I've seen of my land is the North Country. The moors between the towns of Carlisle and Derby. And that in the rain and snow.
Alfieri: Alas!
Charles: Alas, indeed. (*wryly*) But I did see a great deal of Scotland. A very great deal.
Alfieri: A handsome land, too, I believe.
Charles: A man might think so – if he's partial to rock, snow, wet bog, freezing wind and thin black cattle...

> *Charles lapses into a reverie. He mutters to himself, Scotland on his mind. He drinks from his bottle without offering the wine.*

Louise: Ah, but the dramatic stage upon which my Lord acted out his heroic deeds.
Alfieri: As all Europe knows.
Louise: But does all Europe know the role played by Miss Betty Burke?

Alfieri: Miss Betty Burke?

Louise: Unaware of the adventures of Miss Betty Burke? Shame on you, Count Alfieri.

Alfieri: You have me at a disadvantage, Madam.

Charles: (*sheepishly*) What my wife is referring to, Count Alfieri, is my escape from the Island of Lewis to the Island called Skye. Dressed, I must confess it, in the clothes of a lady.

Louise: An Irish lady, to be exact. A maidservant called Betty Burke. (*teasingly*) They say that my lord made a most *fetching* maidservant. Large, but fetching.

Charles: Louise. I'm sure that...

Louise: I've even heard it said that one young boatmen was in love with him. And went so far as to make an indelicate suggestion. In Gaelic, of course, so my lord's blushes were spared.

Charles: (*laughing*) What balderdash!

Louise: Was this boatman so forward as to lay his hands on the Royal Person?.

Charles: If he had, Madam, they'd have been sliced off at the wrist, I can assure you.

Louise: Oh dear. The hazards of love.

Charles: As you can see, Count Alfieri, my wife regards it as her duty to prick what she sees as my inflated dignity. It's a skill at which she excels.

Louise: Thank you, my lord. I try to be of service.

Charles: (*harshly*) What she forgets, however, is that when a man has a Hanoverian bayonet halfway up his arse he thinks little of his dignity. And he's quite prepared to scamper about in skirts if it'll keep his neck off the headsman's block.

Louise: But it's a sight I would have loved to have seen, though.

Charles: What is Madam? My neck on the headsman's block?

Louise: (*laughing*) No, Sire. But the figure of Your Majesty in your female finery. Skirts and petticoats, shawls and stockings. And garters. Did you wear garters, my lord? To keep your stockings up? Or do Highland ladies wear stockings?

Charles: Harrumph.

Louise: (*with a glance at Catherine*) And whatever did you do for a, well, bosom?

> *Louise and Catherine put their heads together in a giggle. Then they sense they have gone too far.*

Charles: Madam. A word of caution.

Louise: My apologies, Sire. But...

Charles: But what?

Louise: I cannot help wondering whether you looked like your ancestor?

Charles: (*he is taken aback*) My ancestor? Which ancestor?

Louise: The Queen. The one who *failed* to keep her neck off the headsman's block. They say she was very beautiful.

Charles: Ah, Mary Stuart. The Queen of Scots.

Louise: Yes, Mary Stuart. Queen of Scots.

Charles: Good God, woman. How should I know whether or not I looked like Mary Stuart?

Louise: She was a big woman, too, was she not?

Charles: So I believe.

Louise: Now *there's* a fit subject for the pen of an ambitious tragedian, Count Alfieri?

Alfieri: Is it, Madam?

Louise: Indeed it is, Sir.

Alfieri: Tell me?

Louise: A young woman, Royal, beautiful, intelligent and a devout Catholic. One of the finest princesses in Europe.

Charles: Or so they say.

Louise: Brought up in the splendour and luxury of the French court. Married to the Dauphin of France, who dies young.

Alfieri: Go on.

Louise: Then, at the age of nineteen – just a girl – she inherits the throne of Scotland.

Charles: Of all places.

Louise: A land in which she's never set foot. A damp, hateful place full of Protestant lords who despise her, and plot against her.

Charles: What else would she expect in Scotland?

Louise: And sharing the same island with another Queen. A powerful English Queen. Who envies Mary's youth and fears her French upbringing and her Catholic faith. And who brings about poor Mary's downfall. After years and years in a castle dungeon

Charles: Not a dungeon. In some comfort, actually.

Louise: Then she is executed. Beheaded.

Alfieri: (*uncertainly*) Ah, yes. It does seem interesting, Madam. Most interesting.

Louise: Interesting? Royalty! Beauty! Betrayal. The death of Queens. It's the very *stuff* of tragedy, Sir.

Catherine: (*simpering*) And I'm sure that Count Alfieri would write it beautifully.

Louise: What do you think, my lord?

Charles: Me? Ah… well…

Louise: Would *you* welcome a tragedy about your ancestor? Elegantly written, as I'm sure it would be, by Count Alfieri? In Italian?

Charles: Ah. Well. Yes. Yes. Why not? The story should be told. For posterity.

Louise: And you, Count Alfieri. Wouldn't you like to learn the story of this beautiful, tragic Queen. But not from some miserable old book, or dusty old text. But from the King of England himself.

Alfieri: (*warily*) That would, of course, be an extraordinary privilege.

Charles: Leave the man be, Louise. Can't you see he's unwilling. I'm sure he's got enough tragedies to be going along with. Eh, Alfieri?

Alfieri: And His Majesty has little enough time, without being plagued by a poet such as myself.

Louise: (*insistently*) Oh, nonsense. I'm sure His Majesty could find time, somewhere in his busy day. In the evenings perhaps, When he's finished with, ah, matters of state. Please say yes, Carlucco. It's such a wonderful story.

Charles: Well... If Alfieri thought it worth his while. I dare say I could find the time. Why not?

Louise: Good. That's settled then. His Majesty will find time for you, Count Alfieri. And if, by chance, His Majesty is detained, or is indisposed, then perhaps I can help. I know a little of the subject.

Charles: (*surprised*) Do you, Madam?

Louise: Yes, Sire, I do.

Charles: Good, good. Mary Stuart it is. See you do her proud, Alfieri. Mary Stuart I mean.

> *He rings the bell.*

Charles: Now I must ask you all to excuse me. There are things I must do. Papers to read. Letters to write. Affairs to manage. That sort of thing.

> *John Stewart enters and helps Charles to his feet. Alfieri gets to his feet and bows low.*

Charles: Pleasure to meet you, Alfieri. I look forward to talking to you again. Most interesting, most interesting. Mary Stuart, eh? I'll do a bit of reading. I'll see what I can remember. Good day to you, Sir.

> *He shuffles off, coughing and wheezing, leaving Alfieri and Louise looking at one another. Alfieri is plainly annoyed.*

Louise: (*mimicking Charles*) Papers to read. Letters to write. Bottles to drink. The man is becoming unsupportable. (*curtly to Catherine*) Catherine, leave us.

> *Catherine quickly leaves the room.*

Alfieri: (*ignoring her tirade*) What are you thinking about, Madam? I don't want to write a play about his damned ancestor.

Louise: Yes you do.

Alfieri: Dammit, I've other things to be getting on with. My own work to do.

Louise: Make Mary Stuart your work.

Alfieri: I've got plays already plotted. Half written. Just waiting to be versified.

Louise: The story of a Mary Stuart is a wonderful story.

Alfieri: That may be. But the history of Europe is littered with wonderful stories.

Louise: Not like the story of Mary Stuart.

Alfieri: Rubbish! Many of them are a damned sight more wonderful than Mary Stuart's.

Louise: The story of Mary Stuart is the finest story in the world.

Alfieri: Why is that?

Louise: (*softly, patiently*) Because, Count Alfieri, it will bring you into the Palazzo Guadagni?

There is a pause as it dawns on Alfieri what she is getting at.

Alfieri: Ah...

Louise: Day after day. Night after night. Month after month.

Alfieri: Ah. There is that.

Louise: Into the house of a man who is drunk most of the time. And who spends many evenings – most evenings – sound asleep?

Alfieri: Asleep, you say?

Louise: Tired out by the great events of his day. Drained of vitality.

Alfieri: A most hard-working monarch.

Louise: And whose wife – whose *young* wife – admires your *poetical* gifts so ardently? Passionately, almost.

Alfieri throws his head back and laughs.

Alfieri: By God, Madam. You're right. The way you tell it, the tragedy of Mary Stuart is a *most* interesting story.

Louise: I thought you'd like it.

Alfieri: I do. I do.

Louise: And, my gallant Count, you should also know that you have swept my lady-in-waiting off her feet.

Alfieri: What?

Louise: Poor dear Catherine is quite overcome by your charms. And who is to blame her?

Alfieri: I don't believe that.

Louise: Yes. It's quite true. And what is more, my lord, you find her very attractive. Very attractive indeed.

Alfieri: (*in amazement*) I find *her*...

Louise: Yes you do. And so far as His Majesty is concerned you now have *two* reasons for visiting the Palazzo Guadagni whenever you can.

Alfieri shakes his head in wonder and laughs.

Alfieri: Your husband may never be the King of England, Madam. But; by God, what a Queen you would have made.

Scene Three

Charles and Louise return from the theatre. They are dressed in their outdoor finery. She is fed up, petulant, moody. She pouts like a spoiled child. She throws herself into a chair and sulks.
Charles settles into his usual chair and rings for Stewart.

Charles: I take it Her Majesty did not enjoy her evening at the theatre.

She does not reply, but turns her head away. Stewart enters.

Stewart: Sir?

Charles: A bottle of Cyprus, Stewart. There's a good fellow.

Stewart: Yes, Sir.

Charles: And *what* did Her Majesty take exception to this time? The acting? Was it the costumes? The music? The dancing?

Louise continues to sulk.

Charles: You surprise me, Louise. It seemed a fair enough little opera to me. I've seen better, I admit. But I've seen worse. I've seen worse.

Stewart comes on with the a bottle and glass. He puts it down on the table beside the Pretender.

Charles: Thank you, Stewart. Well Madam? What was it that provoked such, disdain...?

Louise: I'm tired of the theatre.

Charles: Are you indeed?

Louise: Yes I am.

Charles: A great pity.

Louise: That's all we ever do. Go to the theatre. Walk in the gardens. Or sit here.

Charles: A comfortable enough life, Madam. One that most women would envy.

Louise: Would they?

Charles: And how can this weary life of yours be improved?

Louise: You know, Sir, how it can be improved.

He grows hostile and wary.

Charles: Do I?

Louise: Yes you do.

Charles: We've discussed this before, Louise. Many times. And my answer remains the same.

Louise: (*wheedling*) Oh please, Carlucco. Please.

Charles: You know my feelings on the subject, Madam. It cannot be done.

Louise: But I am a young woman. I need friends. I have no one. I am lonely.

Charles: Am I not company enough?

Louise: I need the company of other women, Carlucco. There are things that only women talk about. I need that.

Charles: And does your lady-in-waiting not suffice for such *têtes a tête*?

Louise: She's only one woman. And an older one at that. No, she is not enough.

Charles and Louise

Charles: Madam, as I have told you a hundred times, every lady in Florence – every lady in Tuscany – is welcome in this Palazzo. You can invite anyone here that you want. At any time.

Louise: (*sulkily*) But they won't come. No one will accept my invitation.

Charles: Then there is nothing I can do about that.

Louise: Yes there is, Carlucco. You know there is.

Charles: There is not.

Louise: Yes there is. The ladies of Florence will not come to this house because I am not permitted to return their calls. It's silly. If you would only allow me...

Charles: (*frostily*) You are the Queen of England, Madam. And the Queen of England does not make calls.

Louise: But Carlucco...

Charles: (*firmly*) No, Madam. No. This house, as you call it, is the English Court. You are its Queen. A Queen does not visit other women, like some kind of, of, I don't know, itinerant midwife.

Louise: (*pleading*) Just a few visits. Discreet ones. Only to some of my closer friends.

Charles: I said no, Madam. No.

Louise: But why?

Charles: Dammit, woman. You *know* why. I've just explained why. And it's the same reason I gave you last time you nagged me about it.

Louise: But Carlucco...

Charles: Royalty does not return house calls. Never. And there's an end to it.

Louise: (*petulantly*) It's not fair.

Charles: (*with some bitterness*) Life is usually unfair.

Louise: (*angrily*) So, I have to go on making do with the theatre do I? My life is to be bounded by all these silly plays and operas and shows. That's all I'm to have, is it? A life hemmed in by tinsel and greasepaint.

Charles: If that's the way you see it, then it would seem so.

Louise: And I'm supposed to forget about everything else that is going on in Florence?

Charles: Everything else?

Louise: All the private balls, and soirées, and concerts and masques and dinner parties that are held all over the city. And to which the King and Queen of England are never invited.

Charles: That is politics, Madam. As you well know. And politics is the price of being Royal.

She sulks some more.

Louise: Well if we're so Royal, why cannot we have a coat of arms over our box at the Pergola?

Charles: (*morosely*) Because the Grand Duke will not allow it, that is why.

Louise: At least that might make the wretched theatre *bearable*. To sit under our own coat of arms. So that the whole world could *see* that we – you and I – are the King and Queen of England.

Charles: Oh, don't be so tiresome, Louise. Is a bit of painted board over our box going to make the acting any better? Or the music more tuneful? Or help the dancers jump any higher?

Louise: It would be *something*.

Charles: It would be nothing.

Louise: It would be a symbol.

Charles: It would be a painted bauble.

Louise: It would be better than what we've got. Which is nothing at all.

Charles: Dammit, woman! You have a Palazzo with fifty servants. You have carriages to take you wherever you want to go. You have more money than you can spend. You have some of the best jewellery in Europe. You are the Queen of England.

Louise: (*muttering*) Of a sort.

Charles: What more do you want?

Louise: I want people to *know* I'm the Queen of England.

Charles: They *do* know.

Louise: And that I am *entitled* to sit under the Royal crest of England. In my own box.

Charles: Well, the Grand Duke has made his feelings plain. No Royal crest. No coat of arms. And he's the master in Tuscany.

Louise: And you're the King of England.

Charles: So they tell me.

Louise: (*wheedling*) Oh Charles, *please*, try again. Petition him. Please...

Charles: (*wearily*) It'll do no good.

Louise: (*firmly*) You must tell him that the dignity of England *demands* a Royal crest in the theatres of Florence.

Charles: He'll not listen.

Louise: Tell him you're insulted.

Charles: I am. I've told him that.

Louise: Then tell him that Tuscany is insulting England.

Charles: I've told him that too.

Louise: Tell him that this cannot go on.

Charles: What am I to do? Send a gunboat up the Arno?

Louise: (*impatiently*) Well, ... oh I don't know. Warn him that the English court might be obliged to withdraw from Florence.

Charles: Oh that *would* strike terror into him.

Louise: He wouldn't like it.

Charles: He'd be delighted. And anyway, where would the English court go? Back to England?

Louise: No. But we could go back to Rome.

Charles: (*coldly*) Back under the heel of the Vatican? On my knees to a Pope who refuses to recognise me as King of England? No Madam, I will not do that.

Louise: So, we remain under the heel of the Grand Duke of Tuscany. Who also refuses to recognise you as King of England. And who insults you – who insults *us* – nightly in the theatres of Florence.

Charles: The Grand Duke takes his cue from the Vatican.

Louise: Then petition the Pope.

Charles: God Madam, you are a tiresome bitch at times.

Louise: Only in Your Majesty's interests.

Charles: And what would I petition the Pope for? To instruct the Grand Duke to allow us to decorate our theatre box in Florence the way we want?

Louise: (*dubiously*) Well, yes.

Charles: That *would* put paid to the Stuart cause. He'd think I'd gone mad. He'd have me locked up.

Louise: (*wailing in frustration*). Then what *can* we do?

Charles: (*bitterly*) Wait for the world to turn, Madam. And have another drink.

Louise: (*in exasperation*) Oh...

> She throws herself into her chair petulantly. He slumps in his gilt chair. He rings the bell for Stewart. Without being asked Stewart brings him another bottle.

Scene Four

Mann and Rudd. Rudd is seated at the desk, Mann is pacing up and down. He is fretful and anxious.

Rudd: (*reading*) Oh this is rich.

Mann: What is?

Rudd: According our friend at Court, the Pretender has turned dramatist.

Mann: (*incredulously*) He's what?

Rudd: So it seems. He's helping Count Alfieri write a tragic drama.

Mann: Good God! What is it about?

Rudd: One of his ancestors. Mary Stuart. The Queen of Scots.

Mann: What the hell does Charles Stuart know about Scottish history?

Rudd: Enough for Alfieri's purpose, I suspect.

Mann: Which is to get his foot in the door.

Rudd: And his cock into the Countess.

Mann: Anything else?

Rudd: Yes. There's a stratagem afoot.

Mann: Is there?

Rudd: Count Alfieri is pretending to be besotted by Mademoiselle de Maltzam while all the time...

Mann: While all the time he's dallying with the Queen of Hearts. Meanwhile the Pretender looks on benignly...

Rudd: Thinking that his wife's loyal lady-in-waiting has found an admirer.

Mann: I wish I'd thought of that one myself. And is it working?

Rudd: It seems to be.

Rudd goes on reading and then bursts out laughing.

Mann: What?

Rudd: How's this. He's had his box at the Pergolà fitted out with a bed.

Mann laughs delightedly.

Mann: A bed? *Do* go on.

Rudd: The poor old bugger's had so much trouble staying awake during the performances...

Mann: Haven't we all...

Rudd: That he's had a bed brought in so that he can just, well, lie down and go to sleep. At the boring bits.

Mann: What an excellent idea.

Rudd: The trouble is, he's a noisy sleeper.

Mann laughs delightedly again.

Mann: You mean he snores.

Rudd: Like a beached whale. Apparently you can hear the old bugger in the gallery.

Mann: (*laughing*) Dear, oh dear, oh dear.

Rudd: Not only does he snore but he groans, moans, coughs, belches and farts as well.

Mann: Do go on.

Rudd: Three nights ago he had to be helped out into the public corridor. Where he was sick on the floor. And all over a lady's shoes.

Mann: I presume his Majestical Folly was drunk?

Rudd: As usual.

Mann: But he's still a regular attender. At the theatrical delights of Florence, I mean.

Rudd: Oh yes. The Stuarts and their little retinue were in attendance last night. 'Amerigo Vespuccio'.

Mann: Which reminds me, I must see that myself. I hear it's rather good. And was the poetical Count Alfieri in attendance?

Rudd: (*glancing at his paper*) Not this time.

Mann: Probably in his lodgings. Chained to his desk. Working on his masterpiece.

Rudd: Maybe. But he's still finding time to write poems.

Mann: To the Queen of Hearts?

Rudd: Who else?

Mann: Show me.

> *Rudd hands him the sheet.*

Mann: (*scans it quickly*). Oh, I say. This is a bit strong isn't it?

Rudd: It hits the mark if you ask me.

> *Mann rises and starts to declaim in an exaggerated fashion.*

Mann: 'O lady, is my fear for thee displeasing
　　　When my warm love is half compact of fear?
　　　Since I beheld thee forced with grief unceasing
　　　The harsh yoke of an aged spouse to bear
　　　Like some trapped dove in vain for mercy pleading
　　　From hands so impious, and from home so drear.'

Rudd: Sounds about right.

Mann: Alfieri wrote this?

Rudd: So our friend says.

Mann: Mmmm. Listen to this. This *is* interesting.

> *He goes on declaiming*

Mann: 'I mean to snatch thee, my alarm increasing
　　　With each foul act, with every falling tear.
　　　Thou art a damask rose, pure, fresh and blooming,
　　　Crushed in the fingers of a filthy clown...'
Now would that not bring a tear to the hardest eye?

Rudd: No.

Mann: Unfeeling wretch. '... a damask rose, pure fresh and blooming, crushed in the fingers of a filthy clown...' Not Dante Alighieri exactly. But I've heard much worse.

Rudd: I defer to your judgement.

Mann: Of course you do. And so you should. But I must say I am much intrigued by the notion of the good Count *snatching* his, ah, damask rose from the fingers of the, what was it?

Rudd: Filthy clown.

Mann: Yes. The filthy clown. Perhaps he should be encouraged in that, ah, ambition?

Rudd: Why not?

Mann: Let's bend our minds to it. Oh! By the way. What news from the trapped dove's laundry basket?

Rudd: All is bloody.

Mann: Then fortune favours the prurient. As ever.

They both laugh.

Scene Five

Charles and Louise. They are sitting alone in the palace. Louise is reading assiduously. He is drinking, as usual. He is bored. There is a pile of books on the table before him. He flicks idly through the pages. He is, perhaps, slightly drunker than usual, and gets drunker as the scene goes on.

Charles: We're expecting Count, eh, whatsisname, Count Alfieri this evening, are we? The one who's doing Mary Stuart? The poet?

Louise: Yes. I believe so.

Charles: I like Alfieri, you know. He's not your usual kind of poet. Not the mincing nancy that most of them are. He's been around a bit. Done a few things. I like a man who's seen a bit of life.

Louise: They tell me he has the makings of a good tragedian. Maybe even a great one.

Charles: Who tells you?

Louise: People who know about such things.

Charles: Oh well. That's good. I'd hate to cast pearls before swine.

Louise: Pearls?

Charles: My ancestors, Madam. The scions of the Stuart race.

Louise: Oh, I see. And was Mary Stuart one of the Stuart pearls, Carlucco?

Charles: So they say. I'm not so sure. I don't think she handled the Scots too well.

Louise: Perhaps she was too young. With a head full of a young woman's dreams and ambitions.

Charles: Dreams?

Louise: Dreams that could never be realised. Young women have dreams like that.

Charles: Do they?

Louise: Most of them.

Charles: If you say so, my dear. If you say so.

Louise: Even some not-so-young women. Catherine's head is full of them.

Charles: Full of what?

Louise: Dreams, Carlucco.

Charles: Is it? What about?

Louise: Count Alfieri, of course. She blushes every time she lays her eyes on him.

Charles: Does she? Can't say that I noticed.

Louise: Well she does.

Charles: Isn't she a bit, well, old for Alfieri?

Louise: Carlucco! What do a few years matter between two people. And who should know that better than you and I?

Charles: *(disbelievingly)* Hmm. Oh well. I hope she knows what she's doing?

Louise: But I don't want to see her making a fool of herself. Do you think we should discourage him?

Charles: I don't think so. She's a grown woman. Let them sort it out for themselves. (*he cackles*) He can rodger her until he drops, so far as I'm concerned.

Louise: (*with a show of reluctance*) Sir, please.

Charles: My apologies.

Louise: But you're probably right. I just don't want to see her hurt. She's been a loyal friend.

> *He belches noisily, then shifts in discomfort, wincing as he does. His backside is plainly bothering him. She looks away in disgust.*

Charles: Forgive me. Something I've eaten, I fear. It's caused something of an uproar in the Royal gut. Damned uncomfortable, believe me.

Louise: Then perhaps less wine…?

Charles: Nonsense. Good Cyprus wine is the best thing for an uneasy belly. Any doctor will tell you that.

Louise: If my Lord says so.

> *John Stewart enters to announce Alfieri.*

Stewart: Count Vittorio Alfieri, Your Majesty.

> *Alfieri enters and makes his obeisances.*

Alfieri: Your Majesty, Your Majesty.

Charles: (*expansively*) Good evening Alfieri. Good to see you again. Sit down, sit down. Stewart…

Stewart: Your Majesty?

Charles: A wineglass for the Count. And fetch another bottle.

Louise: Oh, and Stewart. Would you ask Mademoiselle de Maltzam to join us, please.

Stewart: Yes Madam.

Charles: I trust you'll take some wine, Alfieri.

Alfieri: I will, Sire. Thank you.

Charles: Good man. I dislike to drink alone. My wife is very abstemious, you know. Hardly a drop passes those lips.

Alfieri: Beauty such as your wife's, Sire, deserves to be zealously guarded.

Charles: You see her as beautiful, do you?

Alfieri: What man wouldn't?

> *Stewart returns with a bottle and glass. Alfieri fills the glass. Catherine comes in and simpers at him. He smiles.*

Alfieri: Your very good health, Madam. And yours, Mademoiselle.

Catherine: Thank you, Count Alfieri. You are kind.

Charles: (*with a cackle*) Is that what ye call it?

> *John Stewart enters with yet another bottle which he stands on the table beside Charles. Charles tops up his glass without offering any more to Alfieri.*

Alfieri: I've been trying to understand how many generations Mary Stuart is removed from Your Majesty?

Charles: Generations? Let me think. (*he puzzles*) Now. My grandfather was James the Second, is that right?

Louise: Yes.

Charles: And he was the one driven out of England in 1688? Am I correct?

Louise: (*patiently*) Yes, Your Majesty.

Charles: So *his* father, Charles the First, was my great-grandfather.

Louise: Also correct.

Charles: Which makes James the First, Mary's son, my great-great-grandfather...

Louise: And Mary Stuart herself your great-great-great-grandmother.

Charles: Yes. That's right. I think.

Louise: What a lot of greatness.

Charles: So, is that clear to you, Alfieri?

Alfieri: As clear as it will ever be, Sire. And is there any family, how shall I say, *understanding* of her?

Charles: Understanding? How do you mean?

Alfieri: Something that might not be in the history texts. Some key to the mystery of her character.

Charles: Was her character mysterious?

Alfieri: Well, she's been much imagined. That always lends a character a mystery.

Charles: Does it? If you say so. You're the poet. There are rumours, of course. Probably started by drunken courtiers. Or gossiping women.

Louise: Or drunken women and gossiping courtiers.

Alfieri: (*laughing*) True.

Charles: Her problem, I suppose, was that she was a fanatical Catholic in a land of fanatical Protestants.

Alfieri: (*smoothly*) A pearl in the oyster.

Charles: Or gristle in the meat. She tried to accommodate them but she couldn't. Perhaps she was cursed. Perhaps we're all cursed. All the Stuarts.

Louise: Why would she be cursed?

Charles: As a fornicator. An adulterer. There were whispers of that.

Louise: (*intrigued*) Were there? I didn't know that. With who?

Charles: What's his name? Her secretary of state? Damn it, I had it in my head a second ago. An Italian fella. David Rizzio!

Louise: Ah yes! Of course. (*excited*) The one who was butchered by her husband.

Charles: Her husband and twelve others.

Louise: Was he killed because he was an adulterer?

Charles: That's one of the stories. The other is that he was killed because the Scots lords – including Mary's husband – were jealous of his political power.

Alfieri: That seems more likely.

Charles: Another story has it that they suspected Rizzio of being the Pope's man.

Alfieri: Was he?

Charles: He could have been. The Pope's reach is long. As I know to my cost.

Alfieri: Sir?

Charles: I thought all Europe knew the story. The Popes, Count Alfieri, have refused to recognise me as King of England.

Alfieri: Ah... Yes. Of course.

Charles: My poor old father was hardly stiff in his grave before they'd stripped the Stuart Palazzo in Rome of England's Royal coat-of-arms. Gone overnight. For all the world knew it could have been the local knocking shop. Bastards!

Alfieri: A grave injustice, I'm sure.

Charles: And an insult. When His so-called Holiness finally granted me an audience, he kept me waiting for an hour, spoke to me for no more than ten minutes, and then made me stand.

Alfieri: Stand, Sire?

Charles: Yes. Stand. The King of England. Hopping from foot to foot like some kind of wretched schoolboy. In front of this mewling old sodomite in a white frock. Ach! Don't talk to me of Popes...

Alfieri: So. You think the Scots lords suspected this Rizzio of being the Pope's man.

Charles: Probably. (*with a sudden cackle*) Or maybe the dirty dogs just lusted after Mary themselves. Fancied dabbling in the Royal backside, if you'll forgive me ladies. And were jealous of Rizzio's bedtime jousting.

Louise: (*glancing at Alfieri*) A Stuart monarch, cuckolded by an Italian. Dear, dear. This David Rizzio. Is it possible then that Your Majesty himself might...

    Charles holds up his hand.

Charles: No, Madam! There are some things that cannot be speculated upon.

Louise: Come Sir. There is only us...

Charles: Not even in private. Do I make myself clear?

Louise: But, Sir...

Charles: No, Madam. No!

Louise: (*resignedly*) As you say, Sire.

    Charles is now well and truly drunk. He tops his glass without regard to Alfieri. He never hesitates to belch. His eyelids grow heavy and he snatches little dozy moments.

Alfieri: And then Mary's husband Darnley was himself killed, was he not?

Charles: (*blinking awake*) What?

Alfieri: Mary's husband. He was killed too.

Charles: Yes. That's right. Blown to pieces. (*he cackles again*) Scattered all over the countryside, the poor bastard. Probably by Bothwell.

Alfieri: Bothwell?

Charles: At least I think it was Bothwell. The man who became Mary's second husband. I think. Yes, that's right.

    He belches and grunts and rubs at his stomach. He clutches his belly.

Charles: (*moaning in agony*) Oh, God. Mother of Christ. My guts. My poor bloody tripes.

Louise: Perhaps it was Mary herself?

Charles: (*still clutching himself*) Mary herself? What do you mean?

Louise: Perhaps Mary Stuart set the bomb that killed her husband?

Charles: (*wincing in pain*) Ah... Why in God's name would Mary want to kill her husband?

Louise: Revenge.

Charles: Revenge? What revenge?

Louise: Revenge for her Italian lover.

Charles: Italian lover? What Italian lover?

Louise: David Rizzio.

Charles: Why are you so determined on this Italian lover, Madam?

Louise: I'm not...

Charles: Is there something about Italian lovers that intrigues you? Is that it?

Louise: No Sir.

Charles: Do you have some *experience* of Italian lovers? Is that what agitates you?

Alfieri: (*intervening hastily*) But you think it was Bothwell, Sire?

Charles: (*scowling at Louise*) Bothwell?

Alfieri: Who killed Mary Stuart's husband?

Charles: Bothwell. Yes. I'm sure of it. Bothwell disposing of a rival. Affairs of state. The politics of power, y'see. The real world.

Alfieri: Yes, most plausible.

Charles: And not out of revenge for some little Italian lover, for God's sake. Revenge...

Louise: Sir...

Charles: Sometimes I think women *think* with their cunts, Alfieri. And Queens are no exception to that rule. That's as true of Mary Stuart as it is of...

Louise: Sir, please.

Charles: Bitches, the lot of them. Useless bitches. Good for only one thing...

> *He begins to doze off. Then he wakes with a start, chuckling to himself.*

Charles: (*blearily*) Politics is not for them, you see, Alfieri.

Alfieri: Not for who, Sir?

Charles: Women, Sir. Women. The only politics they understand is the politics of the pudenda.

Alfieri: (*embarrassed*) Ah. I see.

Charles: (*cackling*) That's good. You can write that down. The politics of the pudenda. I must remember that one...

> *Chuckling to himself his eyes get heavy and he begins to fall asleep. There is a long silence. He snores faintly.*
>
> *Louise turns to Catherine and dismisses her with an imperious gesture. Catherine scuttles off.*

Alfieri: His Majesty seems, well, tired by his literary exertions.
Louise: Great events take their toll. Even on the strongest of men. The poor, dear, King.

> *She gets up and walks behind Charles' chair. She takes his head in her hands. The contempt on her face is plain. He stirs fitfully and half-wakens.*

Louise: Hush, my lord. Hush…
Charles: Alfieri, you still there?
Alfieri: Yes, Sire.
Charles: Good. Yes. We'll talk again… some other time… I'm tired now…

> *He falls back into a drunken sleep. This time his sleep is sound. Louise stands behind his chair, smiling bitterly. Alfieri gazes at the sleeping Charles, and shakes his head. Then he looks at Louise.*

Louise: Are you learning much, Count Alfieri?
Alfieri: A great deal, Your Majesty.
Louise: I'm glad. As my lord has made plain, the lot of a Queen – any Queen – is not an easy one.
Alfieri: He's made that *very* plain.

> *Alfieri moves closer to her. The scene becomes intimate. Their voices drop.*

Louise: But you're finding this instructive? This tale. This tragedy?
Alfieri: The more I learn, the more I pity the poor lady. The poor Queen.

> *He takes her hands.*

Louise: She deserves much sympathy, Count Alfieri.
Alfieri: And she has all the sympathy I have to offer, Your Majesty.
Louise: Does she?
Alfieri: And my admiration.

> *They kiss gently. Then with more enthusiasm.*

Louise: A consolation to any Queen.

> *With a quiet laugh Louise takes Alfieri by the hand and leads him off the stage. The Pretender goes on sleeping in his chair. The empty bottle rolls on the floor. John Stewart enters and picks it up. He looks at the sleeping Stuart, looks off-stage to where the couple disappeared, and shakes his head.*

Scene Six

Mann and Rudd. Mann is in his wheelchair, trying it out, spinning around the room.

Mann: Tell me Rudd. What d'ye think of my new go-cart? Good eh? Specially made, you know. For my second infancy. Well sprung. Good wheels. Runs like silk.

Rudd: Very nice.

Mann: The Florentines are good at this sort of thing don't you think? The glories of the Renaissance were not in vain. There is art, and there is art.

Rudd: Maybe if you paid some attention to your doctors you wouldn't need such a contraption.

Mann: Pshaw! What do doctors know. They cup you and leech you and charge you the earth. Licensed to damn you and rob you at one and the same time. Once a man has the gout all he can do is nurse it, and buy himself a go-cart.

Rudd: Whatever you say.

Mann: And remind himself that the great Cosimo de Medici himself was a martyr to it. The brotherhood of the goutish is exalted. Have you met with our friend?

Rudd: I have.

Mann: And how *are* things at the Court of the King and Queen of Fairies?

Rudd: Squalid.

Mann: Oh, I say. Do go on.

Rudd: He's drinking more Cyprus than ever. He's often sick. He has dizzy spells, fainting fits and at least one apoplexy. The laudanum he takes does not help. His tripes are in a constant uproar. He farts non-stop. And the word is that he is pissing blood. Probably shits it too.

Mann: Poor man.

Rudd: His legs are swollen. And the doctors can do nothing about the running sores. He has a dropsy on his chest. He can't breathe without wheezing. He has trouble sleeping. In short, Sir Horace, the man's a wreck.

Mann: Is he dying?

Rudd: No he's not dying. Just disintegrating.

Mann: Ah, the frailty of the flesh. He used to be *such* a handsome young man, you know. A real beauty, in his Stuart way. One of the prettiest heads in Italy.

Rudd: If you say so.

Mann: I do, I do. But, alas, *tempus fugit*. For us all, I fear. And how goes milady's liaison with her poet.

Rudd: Closer by the minute.

Mann: We're sure about that, are we?

Rudd: Aye. He's at the Palazzo Guadagni every night. They talk. They play music. They sing together. They discuss poetry. They consider the works of Montaigne.

Mann: Now there's a nice irony. The aspiring Queen of England and the prophet of the ordinary. Strange bedfellows. Talking of which...

Rudd: Yes, they are.

Mann: No doubt about that?

Rudd: None. And if the Pretender had been sober he would have noticed weeks ago. Or so I'm told.

Mann: Perhaps he doesn't care that his wife is, ah, how shall I say...

Rudd: Dancing on the end of another man's cock. He would if he knew. Apparently the old bugger has barricaded her bedroom.

Mann: He's what?

Rudd: It's true. He's barricaded her bedroom. The only way into her room is now through his. The other entrance is blocked with chairs, stools, chests, tables. Everything he could lay his hands on. It's impenetrable.

Mann: Good God!

Rudd: Not only that. But this great pile of lumber is strung all over with thread. With little bells attached. If anyone touches it – or even comes near it – the bells sound.

Mann: (*laughing*) Ah, me. The chimes of sin. The bells of hell. So where do they do their, ah...?

Rudd: Fornicating?

Mann: I was *going* to say courting. But if that's the word you prefer, who am I to object?

Rudd: Wherever they can, it seems. In pantries, In corridors. Behind curtains. Under the stairs. Out in the garden if the weather's fine. It's a big house. And anyway the old fellow's asleep half the time.

Mann: Do the servants know what's going on?

Rudd: Most of them.

Mann: But nothing has got back to Stuart?

Rudd: Not yet, it seems.

Mann: (*shaking his head*) What a very strange household.

Rudd: Stranger than we know.

Mann: And the play? How goes Count Alfieri's famous play? The one that the Pretender himself has inspired.

Rudd: The first results are expected any day now.

Mann: Are they? Well, I do hope the Count's efforts are successful. A nice tragedy about Mary, Queen of Scots might be just the thing to, well, brighten up our evenings.

Rudd: And give us all a good laugh.

The two men laugh comfortably.

Act II

Scene One

The Palazzo Guadagni. Charles, Louise and Catherine. Louise is strumming idly on a guitar or lute. Catherine is working at her embroidery. Charles is slumped in his chair, sound asleep. His swollen, bandaged leg is propped up on a footstool. As he sleeps he snores and sputters. There is a bottle at his side. He belches and farts.

Catherine: His Majesty is restive this evening.

Louise: His Majesty is restive every evening. And every night. And he's getting worse.

Catherine: Is he?

Louise: He moans and groans. He twists and turns like some kind of, I don't know, trapped beast. He talks in his sleep. Sometimes he shouts and swears. He throws his arms about. Every morning there are new bruises on my arms and legs. Look...

Louise raises her skirts to demonstrate the bruises on her legs. She pulls her gown off her shoulder to show her upper arm.

Catherine: (*wincing*) My poor Lady.

Louise: Poor Lady, indeed. But the worst thing is the smell. Oh God, the smell. He has colic all the time. I think his bowels are collapsing. He spends half the night sitting on his commode. Then he expects me to sleep with him in the stink.

Catherine: (*shocked*) Madam. I don't know what to say. It's a heavy burden for a young wife.

Louise: It's a heavy burden for any wife. Young or old. (*she sniffs the air*) Oh, mother of God. He's farted again.

The women edge their chair away from the sleeping Charles. Louise suddenly giggles.

Louise: The man's a walking cannonade. He delivers a twenty-gun salute for every bottle he drinks.

Catherine: (*calculating*) That's, ah, almost two hundred guns a day.

Louise: At the very least. (*she giggles suddenly*) If I'm the Queen of Hearts, then His Majesty must be the King of Farts.

They giggle together.

Catherine: The Queen of Hearts and the King of Farts. That sounds like an aria from an opera at the Pergolà.

Louise: Or a poem. (*she recites*)

        The Queen of Hearts and the King of Farts
        Went to Florence together.

Catherine: ... When they got there

Louise: ... The Cupboard was bare

Catherine: ... So they ran around in a dither.

They laugh at their efforts. Louise glances at Charles and they shush one another.

Louise: That's very poetic. Let's do another. You go first.
Catherine: The Queen of Hearts and the King of Farts
                     Walked out in the Streets of Venice
                     Said He to she...
Louise: Ah... I need a pee
                     So please hold on to my penis.

They collapse in laughter. Charles stirs and grunts in his sleep. They shush one another. They don't want him awake to spoil the fun.

Catherine: Madam! That's disgraceful. Where *did* you learn such words?
Louise: From my husband's library. It's very large. His library I mean.

They giggle again.

Louise: You go this time.
Catherine: Ah... The Queen of Hearts and the King of Farts
Louise: ... Had nowhere to lay their head
Catherine: ... So they said to Rome
                     We're going home
Louise: ... And Rome said (*in a deep voice*) not till you're dead.
       And that's not so funny.
Catherine: No, Madam.
Louise: All right. One more. Just one more.
Catherine: The Queen of Hearts and the King of Farts
Louise: ... Went to Rome one day
Catherine: ... They said to the Pope
Louise: (*bleakly*) ... Give us some rope
                     And we'll hang ourselves while you pray.

There is a silence.

Catherine: I think we should stop now.
Louise: I suppose so.

John Stewart enters.

Stewart: Count Alfieri, Your Majesty.

Alfieri bustles in carrying a wad of papers. He bows.

Alfieri: Good day, Your Majesty. Mademoiselle de Maltzam.
Louise: Good day, Count Alfieri.
Catherine: Good day to you, Sir.
Alfieri: I see that His Majesty is, ah...
Louise: Resting, Sir. Resting after an arduous day. As all his days are, poor
       King.
Alfieri: A pity. I have some scenes from Mary Stuart that might be of interest
       to him.
Louise: I'm sure they would be.

She gets up, walks behind his chair and twists both Charles's ears. He sputters awake, rubbing his face, not sure what has happened to him.

Charles: What... Madam...

Louise: Count Alfieri is here, Sire.

Charles: Who? Who's here...?

Louise: Count Alfieri is here. With something for you.

Charles: Something for me. Who has? Oh. Alfieri. Yes. How d'ye do. Sit down, sit down.

Alfieri: Your Majesty.

> *Charles reaches for his bottle and glass. Finds the bottle empty and rings for Stewart. Stewart replenishes the tray. Charles replenishes his glass.*

Charles: What d'ye have for me?

Alfieri: A few scenes from Mary Stuart.

Charles: Mary Stuart? Oh, the *play*. The tragedy. Yes, right. Good, good. That's good.

Alfieri: It's not finished, of course.

Charles: No, no. Too soon, of course.

Alfieri: But it's well under way. Thanks to Your Majesty's help.

Charles: (*magnanimously*) Glad to be of some use to somebody. It's going well, is it?

Alfieri: I think so. I hope so.

Charles: That's good.

Alfieri: I was hoping that Your Majesty would like to hear a few lines. If you are not too fatigued...

Charles: Only too delighted.

Alfieri: Thank you, Sir.

Charles: There's nothing in what you've written down that might offend the ladies is there? I wouldn't want that.

> *For some reason Louise and Catherine find this amusing. They laugh. Charles is faintly puzzled. Then decides that women are too mysterious to fathom.*

Alfieri: No, Sire. Nothing.

Charles: Right then, Alfieri. Let's hear what you've got.

Alfieri: Well, Sir. I must tell you that I am much taken by the figure of Mary's husband.

Charles: Who? Bothwell?

Alfieri: No, her first husband. Henry Stewart, the Earl of Darnley.

Charles: Ah, yes. My other ancestor. The one that was blown to pieces in Edinburgh. Ever seen a man blown to pieces, Alfieri? Or had his head lifted off by a cannon ball?

Alfieri: No, Sire.

Charles: (*morosely*) Didn't think you had. I have. More than once. It's not something I want to see again, to tell you the truth.

Alfieri: (*ignoring him*) I see Darnley as a man who does not know how to accept his fate. A man who cannot reconcile himself to being Mary Stuart's consort. A King but not quite a King.

Louise: A nearly monarch.

Charles: (*suspiciously*) Yes. I can see that would have been difficult for him.

Alfieri: Particularly as the other Lords seem to have envied his power. And spied on him. And plotted against him.

Charles: (*sourly*) They were Scots, weren't they.

Louise: Carlucco! Such a thing to say about your loyal Scots.

Charles: There are Scots, Madam, and there are Scots. While one's at your side, the other's at your throat. A skittish breed, the Scots. A horse-lover like Alfieri knows what I'm talking about. Eh, Sir?

Alfieri: Ah, yes. Yes of course.

Charles: (*morosely*) Not that the English are any better. Worse if anything. They're *all* Hanoverians now. Or so the Hanoverians think.

Louise: (*impatiently*) Then thank God for the Irish.

Charles: As you say. Thank God for the Irish. Good Catholics to a man. Pity they're too few to be useful. And too ignorant.

Alfieri: So, Sire. With your permission.

Charles: Please. Go ahead.

> *Charles slips into a semi-doze. Alfieri prepares to read. He gets up from his chair and starts to walk about.*

Alfieri: (*to Louise*) I wonder if Your Majesty would honour me by reading a little of the Queen's part?

Louise: May I, Carlucco?

Charles: (*still in a reverie*) May you what?

Louise: Count Alfieri would like me to read a little of Queen Mary's part. May I?

Charles: Queen Mary's part?

Louise: In his play.

Charles: Oh I see.

> *He pours himself a drink from his ever-present bottle and stares at Alfieri reflectively.*

Charles: (*vaguely displeased without knowing why*) Oh, go ahead. Read on, Madam. Read on. If it amuses you.

Louise: Thank you, Sire. (*she stands up and drops him a curtsy*) I hope I'll be worthy of your great ancestor.

Charles: (*he chortles*) Just see that you don't lose your head.

Alfieri: Now, Madam. If you would just stand here. I'll stand here.

Charles: What's the scene?

Alfieri: It's a little scene from Act Three, Sir. I play the part of Henry Stewart, Lord Darnley. Mary's husband.

Charles: And consort.

Alfieri: Exactly. She is trying to reassure him that the great difference in their ranks is of no consequence.

Charles: A reassuring wife. A touching scene, indeed.

Alfieri: I hope so, Sir.

Charles: Go on then, go on.

Louise: Where do I start?

Alfieri: From where it says, 'Thou'rt welcome here'.

Louise: I hope you understand, Count Alfieri, that I'm no actress.

Charles: (*sarcastically*) Some of us would regard you as a most accomplished actress, Madam.

Louise: Thank you, Carlucco. You are kind.

Charles: Am I? Oh.

Louise: Most of the time.

Alfieri: Now, Madam. Just speak the words slowly. Don't rush them. But not too slow.

Charles: A good steady pace, eh.

Alfieri: As His Majesty says. A good steady pace.

> *Louise clears her throat nervously. Alfieri watches her anxiously. Charles seems to doze off again. His head droops. Louise begins to recite Alfieri's words. The language is florid and old-fashioned. Her voice is stilted and goes up a register.*

Louise: 'Thou'rt welcome here, thou whom as the inseparable partner of all my griefs and joys I chose. At last, thou yieldest, and dost listen to my prayers.'

Alfieri: Slower, Madam. Slower. Somewhat more, ah, meaning in the words.

Charles: As if you really love him.

Alfieri: Exactly, Sir.

Louise: Will I start again?

Alfieri: Yes, please.

Louise: 'Thou'rt welcome here, thou whom as the inseparable partner of all my griefs and joys I chose. At last, thou yieldest, and dost listen to my prayers.'

Charles: Prettily said, Louise.

Louise: 'At length within thy palace thou returnest. That it's always thine thou knowest well. Although in voluntary banishment, from thence it pleases thee to live so far.'

Charles: What voluntary banishment? I don't recall any banishment. Voluntary or otherwise.

Alfieri: Just a little of the poet's license, Your Majesty. For the sake of dramatic effect.

Charles: Oh. (*mumbles*) Dramatic effect, eh...

Louise: 'Although in voluntary banishment, from thence it pleases thee to live so far.

Alfieri: 'Queen...'

Louise: 'Why thus call me? Why not call me consort?'

> *Charles begins to snore. Louise and Alfieri look at him and then at one another.*

Alfieri: 'Say, are our destinies the same?'

Louise: 'Ah, no. Thou mak'st me spend my tedious days in tears.'

Alfieri: 'My tears thou seest not.'

Louise: 'I have beheld thee, bedew, 'tis true... '

Charles comes awake with a little start. He's been listening, or at least half-listening.

Charles: Beheld thee what? Bedew, 'tis true?

Louise: Bedew, Carlucco. As in the dew that drops on the grass. In the mornings.

Charles: Oh *that* dew. The wet kind.

Louise resumes her recitation.

Louise: I have beheld thee, bedew...

Charles: I thought you meant the other kind. The moneylending kind.

He cackles and then he groans and belches. There is a silence.

Charles: You'll all have to forgive me. Not feeling very sprightly this evening. Not too well...

Charles begins to doze again.

Alfieri: So! Where were we?

Louise: Go back to 'ah, no'.

Alfieri glances at Charles.

Alfieri: Is His Majesty...?

Louise shakes her head and grimaces. The gesture means 'ignore him'.

Louise: 'Ah, no. Thou mak'st me spend my tedious days in tears.'

Alfieri: 'My tears thou seest not.'

Louise: 'I have beheld thee, bedew, 'tis true thy cheek with tears of rage. But not of love.'

As they talk their voices become lower and more meaningful. They move closer to one another. They are Mary Stuart and Henry Darnley, in love.

Alfieri: 'Whatsoever be the cause, I wept. And still I weep.'

Louise: 'And who can cure this ceaseless grief, who wipe my tearful eyes, who to my soul restore pure genuine joy, who, if not thou...'

There is loud retching noise as Charles leans over the sofa to be sick. Louise covers her face with her hands in disgust and despair. Alfieri puts his arms round her shoulders to comfort her. She shrugs him away and rushes off, followed by Catherine.

John Stewart comes on to clear up the mess. While Stewart is sorting things out. Alfieri stares at the retching hulk, then goes off leaving Stewart trying to lift Charles to his feet. Stewart talks soothingly to him, as if to a child.

Stewart: Come along now, Sir. Come along. I think the play is over. That's it. There's a good King. There's a good King.

Scene Two

Mann and Rudd. Mann is still in his bath chair. Rudd is seated at the table, being dictated to. Rudd is carrying his notebook. He settles at the table while Mann dictates.

Mann: Where were we?

Rudd: (*reading back*) '... and so weak that he has been supported by two servants from his coach to his box where, as usual, he laid on a couch...'

Mann: Write this. His physician tells me that he thinks a dropsy on his breast is formed, and I am informed by people in his house and by those who frequently dine with him that he has quite lost his appetite...

Rudd: But not his taste for Cyprus, I'll wager...

Mann: ... though he still drinks strong wine.

Rudd: Thought so.

Mann: (*coldly*) Shall we finish the letter, Rudd?

Rudd: Sorry, Sir Horace. Go on.

Mann: Thank you. (*he laughs*) I must inform your Lordship of what will appear a ludicrous circumstance. This poor vision of a man...

Rudd: That's a good one.

Mann: This poor vision of a man has always kept, and still has, under his bed a strong-box with twelve thousand sequins which, he says, he has kept ready for the expenses of his journey to England...

Rudd: Daft bugger.

Mann: ... for the expenses of his journey to England whenever he shall suddenly be called thither. And this your Lordship may depend on. That'll do. Followed by the usual compliments.

Rudd: Does this silly sod *really* believe that the people of England are going to rise up any day now, and topple King George?

Mann: I suppose he must. Why else keep twelve thousand sequins under the bed?

Rudd: Good God. How long has it been since we had Stuarts on the throne?

Mann: Ninety years. Give or take a month or two.

Rudd: (*shaking his head*) Ninety years of delusion and folly.

Mann: And mischief-making, Rudd. Never forget that. Now, then. As you have your pen in your hand, I wonder if you'd oblige me by drafting a letter to our Mister Stuart.

Rudd: To Stuart? What kind of letter?

Mann: A *nasty* kind of letter.

Rudd: Saying what?

Mann: Oh, accusing him of beating and abusing his wife. Telling him that every decent Englishman who visits Florence is shocked...

Rudd: You mean outraged.

Mann: Outraged, indeed. The very word. By the way he treats the poor dear lamb. And is surprised that she remains with him. That kind of thing.

Rudd: Yes, Sir Horace.

Mann: Anonymous, of course.

Rudd: Of course.

Mann: Then, what we'll do is, we'll dispatch it to London And have it sent back to the Palazzo Guadagni from there. Now ask me why.

Rudd: No need. You want Stuart to think that his *scandalous* behaviour to his wife is the talk of London. That polite society in England talks of little else.

Mann: *Exactly*, my dear boy. Exactly. We'll make a diplomatist of you yet.

Rudd: (*not without irony*) Thank you, Sir Horace.

Scene Three

The Palazzo Guadagni. Charles, Louise, Catherine. Charles appears to be in an expansive mood. They are waiting for Alfieri. Stewart enters to announce him.

Stewart: Count Al...

Charles: Aha! Genius needs no announcing, Mister Stewart. It is always welcome at the English court. Majesty, as is proper, defers to genius.

Charles half rises and bows to Alfieri.

Alfieri: (*taken aback and wary*) Sire. I...

Charles: Kings may come and Kings may go, but genius goes on for ever. Am I right, Alfieri?

Alfieri: (*warily*) Your Majesty is kind.

Charles: Not kind, but just. As Kings must be. Sit ye down, Sir, sit ye down. And allow my good and faithful – at least I think he's my good and faithful – Stewart here to pour you a glass of Cyprus. Stewart, do the needful.

Stewart does the needful.

Charles: Tell me Stewart. *Have* you been faithful. To me I mean?

Stewart: Sir?

Charles: Oh, don't look so puzzled, man. You know as well as I do that Sir Horace Mann has his little spies in this household. We all know that, don't we?

Stewart: I have heard that suggested, Sir.

Charles: And?

Stewart: And I can assure Your Majesty that I am not one of them.

Charles: Are you not?

Stewart: No Sir, I am not.

Charles: Never taken King George's shilling?

Stewart: No, Sir.

Charles: Never danced to the tune piped by that mincing oid sodomite Mini Mann?

Stewart: No, Sir.

Charles: And you expect me to believe you?

Stewart: Yes Sir, I do.

Charles: Well, I suppose I do. Anyway what does it matter? What could you tell King George that he couldn't guess for himself. You may go.

Stewart: Thank you, Sir.

Stewart bows and leaves. Louise turns on Charles.

Louise: Sir, that was cruel. And uncalled for. John Stewart has been with you for thirty years...

Charles: Forty.

Louise: You have no reason to suspect him. Or to treat him like that.

Charles: Every time I shit on my pot, Madam, one of Mann's spies is there. Weighing and measuring the turd and sending the results back to King George.

Louise: Charles, please…

Charles: (*shrugging*) But what's a man to do? A King needs his servants. Servants can be bought. Or subverted. It's the way of the world. Treachery and seduction are the currency of our times. Don't ye agree, Alfieri?

Alfieri: There is much in what Your Majesty says.

Charles: Glad you think so. Well, now. Tell me. How does your muse these days, Count Alfieri.

Alfieri: She appears to have withdrawn her favours.

Charles: Oh dear. Louise. D'ye hear that. The poor Count's muse has abandoned him.

Louise: Sad news.

Charles: Fled into the arms of another, has she? I presume there is another?

Alfieri: There's always another, Sire.

Charles: You're right there.

Alfieri: (*hastily*) The muse is courted by more men than I care to imagine.

Charles: And dispenses her favours to them all. The wanton harlot.

Louise: I take it then, that the tragedy of Mary Stuart is going badly.

Alfieri: Well. Shall we say that the tragedy of Mary Stuart is going slowly, Madam. More slowly than I'd hoped.

Catherine: This is a great pity, Sir. What we heard we liked. Did we not, Your Majesty?

Charles: Did we?

Louise: (*sensing trouble*) But a story with some way to go. Before it is finished.

Charles: Oh a long way. I've no doubt it will require many more visits to the Palazzo Guadagni, will it not, Count Alfieri?

Alfieri: (*cautiously*) If Your Majesty will allow it.

Charles: Oh this Majesty will allow almost anything. Unlike other majesties, this Majesty understands art. This Majesty *participates* in the dramatist's creation.

Alfieri: For which, Sire, this dramatist is eternally grateful.

Charles: Other majesties fritter their time away on affairs of state. Leading armies. Fighting wars. Crushing their enemies. Ruling countries. Transient nonsense like that. But not Charles Stuart, King of England. Charles Stuart, King of England, makes *art*…

> *There is an embarrassed silence. Charles looks on them with a savage grin.*

Charles: While his wife…

Louise: (*hastily*) Can only thank the Good Lord for blessing her with a husband of such rare gifts.

Charles: While his wife dallies… with her own muse.

Louise: Currently, Monsieur Michel de Montaigne. Dead these many years.

Charles: Dallying with the dead. A strange business this art, then. But is it enough? Eh? Can the muse *satisfy* a man? What d'ye think, Count Alfieri?

Alfieri: I've always found it so, Sire.

Charles: What? A travelling, venturesome gentleman like yourself. A dashing young Piedmontese horseman. A *bareback rider* like you? Surely not?

Alfieri: (*nervously*) I travel for the sake of my art.

Charles: Ah. You do, do you? And fornicate for the sake of your poetry?

Alfieri: (*taken aback*). Sire?

Louise: Carlucco! Please.

Charles: Oh, come now. We're all men and women of the world here, are we not? You're a young man. With all a young man's enthusiasm for a lady's, ah, moister parts. That's an enthusiasm that any man can understand. And ladies too. If pressed.

Louise: (*coldly*) Sire, your crudity does you no justice.

Charles: (*coldly*) Perhaps not, perhaps not. But it does Count Alfieri more than justice. It credits him with honest lust.

Alfieri: Meaning what, Sire?

Charles: (*coldly*) Meaning, Sir, your taste for other men's wives.

> *There is a stunned and frightened silence. Suddenly Charles is a formidable figure. a menacing hulk that dominates the company.*

Alfieri: Sire, please. I don't know what you mean.

Charles: I mean, Sir, your little pastime of creeping into an honest man's house and debauching his partner.

Louise: Sire, I cannot allow you to insult a guest in this way.

Charles: Insult? Insult my ailing arse.

Louise: Your Majesty! Please?

Charles: Ask your poet and tragedian, about Penelope Ligonier.

> *Louise turns to Alfieri questioningly. Alfieri is in disarray.*

Louise: Who?

Charles: Lady Penelope Ligonier.

Louise: Who was she?

Charles: Ask him.

> *Louise turns to Alfieri. He is silent.*

Charles: Oh. The Piedmontese songbird is mute, is he? Then let me warble for him. Lady Penelope Ligonier was an English Lady. The wife of the Earl of Ligonier. Colonel of the Ninth Regiment of Foot.

Alfieri: (*feebly*) The Lady and I were in love.

Charles: That's what you call it do you?

Alfieri: I do.

Charles: Love. Ah, the drama of it all.

Alfieri: Please...

Charles: The poetry of it. Worming your way, poetically, into the Lady's bed while her husband was away. Sneaking, dramatically of course, into the Earl's country house while he was in London.

Alfieri: The Lady and I were...

Charles: I know, in love. So! While the Colonel was drilling his soldiers you were drilling his wife. Oh, very poetical. Very dramatical. Very Eye-talian.

Louise: (*with some defiance*) Count Alfieri's private affairs are nothing to do
with us.

Charles: I trust not, Madam. I trust not. Tell the ladies about your famous
duel, Count Alfieri.

Alfieri: I will not, Sir.

Charles: Then allow me. Naturally, ladies, the Earl got to hear about the
debauching of his wife. So one evening he marched into the theatre in the
Haymarket – the Italian Opera House wasn't it? – and challenged the bold
Count here to a duel. Where was it, Alfieri? Green Park? Blades at sunset?
Very theatrical.

> *Alfieri is now thoroughly embarrassed and humiliated. The two women
> are staring at him in amazement.*

Charles: Not that it was much of a contest. An English soldier and a
Piedmontese fop like this. Pshaw!

Alfieri: (*angrily*) I had injured my shoulder.

Charles: You see, ladies, cocksman he may be, but swordsman he is not.

Louise: (*miserably*) Your Majesty, please?

Charles: Our poet put up such a miserable display that Ligonier disdained to
spill his Italian tripes on the grass. He told his friends that it would have
been like spitting a baby.

Louise: This is too sordid for words.

Charles: Oh, no. There were plenty of words. More than enough. The stirring
saga of Lady Penelope and Count Alfieri found its way into the public
prints.

> *He brandishes a pamphlet.*

Charles: This print, in fact. Entitled (*he reads*) 'The Generous Husband – or
Lord Laelius and the Fair Emilia'.

Louise: Where did you get *that*?

Charles: From one of my loyal *friends* in London. And damned interesting
reading it makes, may I tell you. It's all here. Chapter and verse. What you
might call a blow by blow account. All set out for the world and his wife
to read.

> *Alfieri is plainly stunned by Charles's onslaught. He tries to recover
> his dignity. He crosses to Louise and bows.*

Alfieri: If you'll forgive me, Madam. I think I should withdraw. To save you
further, ah, embarrassment.

Charles: Oh don't go yet, Count Alfieri. There is more.

Alfieri: Enough, Sir. I beg you.

Charles: Not quite. Not quite. You see my dear, the truly funny thing was that
all the time the Count here was mooning over his Lady Penelope – and no
doubt writing poems to her chaste and wondrous beauty – she was being
rodgered by her husband's coachman. Hah!

Louise: Sire...

Charles: It's true. Isn't it, Alfieri? Every word of it. All the time that she was
being courted by our poet, Lady Penelope was romping in the stables with

a servant. Playing hide the sausage among the bales of hay. Straw in her every orifice.

Louise: Sir, this is intolerable.

Charles: Of course it was. That's why Ligonier divorced the slut.

Louise: (*weakly*) Divorced?

Charles: Oh didn't he tell you? Oh yes. Your poetical hero was cited in a very nasty – and very public – divorce suit. All London was sniggering over it for months.

Alfieri: Sir, Madam, I...

Charles: Of course, Ligonier got his divorce. There was no defence, was there Alfieri? So he threw the Lady Penelope out. Poor Penny was penniless.

Louise: I do not want to hear any more of this.

Charles: But nothing keeps a good whore off her back. The one-time Lady Penelope has now taken up with a strapping young dragoon. And I've no doubt that even as we speak she's being pleasured by his horse.

Alfieri: (*angrily*) Sire, if you were not...

Charles: (*contemptuously*) What now, Count Alfieri? Are you about to call me out? Then have a care, Sir. Old and ill as I am, I still have it in me to gut a Piedmontese poltroon such as you.

Alfieri: (*with as much dignity as he can muster*) Then allow me, *Sir*, to take my leave?

Charles: (*sardonically*) Nothing, Sir, would give me greater pleasure.

> *The two men bow to one another. Alfieri leaves. Louise and Catherine sit ashamed and silenced.*

Charles: Well, Madam. What do you think of your poet and tragedian now?

Louise: (*sullenly and without conviction*) His past is his own affair.

Charles: (*with contempt*) A worm, Madam. A slithering worm. With one object in mind. To find a fresh hole.

Scene Four

Mann and Rudd. Rudd is wheeling Mann in his bath chair.

Mann: I understand that the gallant and gifted Count Alfieri has fallen out of favour.

Rudd: So it seems.

Mann: Ah me! The patrons of great art can be fickle creatures. The Medicis were just the same. I trust the Count has not fled from Florence?

Rudd: No, no. He's still skulking around. Dallying with the Queen of Hearts whenever – and wherever – he can.

Mann: A man of some tenacity. I like that. Did I mention that I saw Mister Stuart perform yesterday.

Rudd: Perform?

Mann: In his role as Charles the Third, King of England by the grace of God...

Rudd: But not by the will of man. What happened?

Mann: It was outside the Uffizi. An old fellow – a beggar by the look of him – came up to him and dropped to his knees. He pleaded to be cured.

Rudd: Of what? The King's evil?

Mann: Presumably.

Rudd: What did the Pretender do?

Mann: Well, he prayed to the sky for a few moments, then took the beggar's face in both his hands, and stroked his cheeks. Three times. Then the beggar kissed his hands. Charles gave him a few coins, and they went their separate ways. Both seemed happy with the transaction. A few people applauded.

Rudd: Superstitious twaddle.

Mann: Maybe. But it was interesting.

Rudd: An ancient folly, that's all.

Mann: More than that I think. It's the power of kingship. This notion that a King – even a derelict old ruin like Charles Stuart – is some kind of enchanted figure that can cure. It's what makes Kings so dangerous.

Rudd: Then wouldn't it be better if we just got rid of him?

Mann: Get rid of him?

Rudd: Yes. Why don't we drop a pistol ball in his ear? Or slip a knife under his ribs. It wouldn't be hard to arrange. A few thousand sequins could see him off.

Mann: Oh dear me. What kind of company *do* you keep Mister Rudd?

Rudd: It's a suggestion.

Mann: And a very bad one, if I may say so.

Rudd: Why?

Mann: Why? Think on it, man. Kill him and he'd be transformed at a stroke. From Charles Edward the Buffoon to Charles Edward the Martyr. From low comedy to high tragedy in one scene.

Rudd: Hmm. Fair point.

Mann: Assassination is the best thing that could happen to him. And to the Stuart cause. In fact, I'm surprised they haven't thought of it themselves.

Rudd: I suppose you're right.

Mann: I am, believe me. No, better the drunken devil we know. Let him shamble around Italy taking umbrage with everybody who forgets to tip their hat to him. Let him pickle his innards in Cyprus wine.

Rudd: He's doing that, all right.

Mann: Good. And if need be, we'll supply him with the four bottles he swigs down every day.

Rudd: Six bottles.

Mann: Six! Good God! Are you sure?

Rudd: So our friend at court says.

Mann: Well, may it soon be ten. That's a nice round figure, I've always thought.

Rudd: Poor bastard.

Mann: (*sardonically*) Pity, Mister Rudd? Minutes ago you were advocating that we – how did it go – drop a pistol ball in his ear.

Rudd: At least that would put the old brute out of his misery.

Mann: Ah, but King George's policy is to keep him *in* his misery.

Rudd: Is it?

Mann: (*coldly*) As I interpret it – yes. To which end, I'd like you to have a word with the loyal Englishmen of Florence.

Rudd: What? All of them?

Mann: Well, the ones you meet.

Rudd: What kind of word?

Mann: Mmmm. Tell them that King George would be grateful if they'd do what they can to discourage the Pretender in his, ah, pretensions. If they happen to bump into him, that is.

Rudd: And how do they do that?

Mann: Oh, nothing violent. Nothing unseemly. Just, well, refuse to acknowledge him at the theatre. Refuse to give way to him on the street. Never touch their hats. Never return a good day, if he offers one.

Rudd: Cut him dead at every turn, eh?

Mann: That's the idea. Perhaps a few hard words or a hiss as they pass him by. The ladies can make do with a little laugh. No shouting, of course. Everything *sotto voce*, as they say at the opera.

Rudd: What kind of unkind words?

Mann: Oh, just whatever takes their fancy. Old fool! Stuart traitor! Popish tyrant!

Rudd: Drunken sot! Renegade! Woman beater!

Mann: That kind of thing. I'm sure it'll have a dispiriting effect in time.

Rudd: I see. Right. I'll pass on King George's instructions.

Mann: Requests, Rudd, requests. The King of England does not instruct. He requests. He's not some kind of Stuart despot, you know.

Rudd: (*sardonically*) Of course he isn't.

Mann: Oh. And do ask His Majesty's subjects *never* to accept an invitation to the Palazzo Guadagni.

Rudd: Aye, Sir Horace.

Mann: That's *very* important. The fewer friends the Pretender has, the happier King George will be. And we do want to keep His Majesty happy, do we not?

Rudd: We do indeed.

Scene Five

The Palazzo Guadagni. It is Saint Andrew's Night, 1780. Charles and Louise on their own. Charles is in one of his strange, bitterly sentimental moods. Drunk of course, but somewhere in the ruins there is a man to be reckoned with.

Charles: I don't suppose you know what day it is?

Louise: What an odd question, Carlucco. Of course I know what day it is. It is the thirtieth day of November.

Charles: Which is?

Louise: Which is Saint Andrew's day.

Charles: Hmm. You remembered.

Louise: How could I forget Saint Andrew?

Charles: Good.

Louise: The patron saint of all wives who keep their legs crossed at the ankles.

Charles: (*quizzically*) What?

Louise: Or if he's not, he should be.

Charles: What in God's name are you talking about, woman?

Louise: I'm talking about Saint Andrew, Carlucco.

Charles: The patron saint of Scotland.

Louise: Oh, he's that too.

Charles: So what do you mean ... ?

Louise: Surely you know the story of Saint Andrew, Carlucco? The saint who cured the Roman Governor's wife of illness. Snatched her back from the edge of the grave, in fact.

Charles: Did he indeed?

Louise: Yes. And she was *so* grateful that she immediately became a pious Christian. A *very* pious Christian.

Charles: And?

Louise: So pious, in fact, that she withdrew her, ah, favours from her husband. Never climbed into his bed again.

Charles: I never knew that.

Louise: Oh yes. And the poor man, well the poor man was so hurt and upset that he blamed Andrew for his wife's, ah, Christian chastity.

Charles: Did he indeed?

Louise: Yes he did. And had the saint crucified. On a cross shaped like a saltire. Which opened the Saint's legs very wide indeed.

Charles: You're raving, Madam. This is all nonsense, surely?

Louise: Not at all, Sir. The story of Saint Andrew and the Roman Governor's wife was one of our little favourites at the Convent at Mons. All the girls used to giggle over it.

Charles: (*sourly*) I'll wager they did. Anyway, anyway. True or not. He's also the patron saint of Scotland.

Louise: Which country – unlike the Roman Governor's wife – was always susceptible to her master's charms.

Charles: Meaning me.

Louise: Meaning that Scotland was always the most loyal part of Your Majesty's mighty realm.

Charles: Part of it was, maybe.

Louise: The best part, I'm sure.

Charles: The worst part, as it happens.

Louise: Oh dear.

Charles: The worst part, but with the best subjects. To whom I raise my glass in toast. And I'll thank you to do the same.

> *They both raise their glasses.*

Louise: To who?

Charles: My loyal Scottish subjects. May the Lord God protect them and save them.

Louise: (*bored*) God bless them all.

> *They drink. Louise resumes her reading.*

Charles: (*grumbling*) That might have been said with a shade more feeling, Madam.

Louise: (*quizzically*) Sir?

Charles: I said that you might have toasted Scotland with more sincerity.

Louise: Carlucco, please. You cannot expect me to share your enthusiasm for people I have never met and a country I have never seen.

Charles: Well you may not know of them, but they know of you. D'ye know what they call you in Scotland?

Louise: No I do not.

Charles: Louisa Horne. That's what they call you. Louisa Horne.

Louise: Very respectful.

Charles: There's a toast, you see. One that they drink to me. It goes... how does it go? Oh yes. 'God bless and reward the lad that's been so kind to Louisa Horne...'

Louise: (*disdainfully*) Very loyal, I'm sure.

Charles: Yes, Madam, they are. And it's a quality I would expect you to appreciate.

Louise: (*bored*) Yes, Sire.

Charles: Dammit woman! Thirty thousand pounds! That was the price on my head. Thirty thousand good English pounds. A King's ransom. Literally.

Louise: Yes Sir. You have mentioned it before.

Charles: Can you *imagine* what money like that would have meant to some of these poor Highland people? Can you imagine?

Louise: (*still bored*) Yes, Sire.

Charles: And not one of them gave me away. Not one! No matter how poor they were. No matter how little they had to eat. No matter that they didn't have a roof over their heads or rags for their back. No matter. They never gave me away.

Louise: Admirable.

Charles: And that, Madam, is what I call loyalty.

Louise: It is one of Your Majesty's best-loved stories. Everyone who has heard it admires it.

Charles: (*suspiciously*) Heroism is always worth recounting, Madam.

Louise: Indeed. It is the stuff of legend, Sir.

Charles: (*brooding*) Damn it, they were hard days. Hungry days. Wet days. Miserable days. God knows why I didn't die.

Louise: God knows.

Charles: Maybe I should have done.

Loulse: Sir. You frighten me when you talk like that.

Charles: D'ye know what I lived on?

Louise: Do remind me.

Charles: Crabs, Madam, crabs. Creeping, green, bloody shore crabs. Boiled over a fire when it was safe. Raw when it wasn't. And dead fish. And mussels. And – when I was lucky – some spoiled oatmeal and some rancid butter.

Louise: Alas, poor King. The very thought makes me shudder.

Charles: (*still brooding*) If you'd seen me then, Madam, you'd never have married me.

Louise: Some things are too hard to believe.

Charles: Hardly a fit consort for a scullery maid. Dressed in rags. Covered in sores, bleeding at the gums. And moving with lice.

   Louise affects a shudder.

Louise: Oh, dear.

Charles: Aye, lice, Madam. Companies of them. Battalions of them. Armies of them. If I'd taken my britches off they'd have marched off without me.

Louise: The thought disgusts me.

Charles: What does?

Louise: The lice, Sir. The lice.

Charles: I certainly disgust myself when I think on it. But – here's the thing – the Hanoverians never found me. Never. Thousands of the bastards, swarming all over Scotland and they never found me. Oh, I led them a dance, I can tell you.

Louise: You have, Sire.

Charles: Have what?

Louise: Told me.

Charles: Have I?

Louise: (*still bored*) But God and the Blessed Virgin be thanked that Your Majesty was spared. To live a long and fruitful life.

Charles: I'm not so sure about the fruitful. (*he lapses into brooding*) I wonder what they'd have done with me if they'd taken me.

Louise: That does not bear thinking about.

Charles: Put me on trial and then shortened me by a head, I suppose.

Louise: They wouldn't have dared.

Charles: Oh yes they would. By God I can see the scene now. The axeman holding me up by the hair. 'Behold, the head of the traitor Charles Stuart'.

Louise: Charles, please…

Charles: With the so-called Duke of Cumberland sitting on the balcony in Whitehall, smirking all over his fat German face.

Louise: You know how I hate such things.

Charles: Well, at least I denied the poltroon that particular pleasure.

Louise: A bloody people, the English.

Charles: (*brooding*) Maybe, maybe. They certainly put an end to many a good Jacobite.

Louise: Sometimes loyalty to a King has its price.

Charles: Aye. That's true enough.

Louise: It's a pity that so few were prepared to pay it.

Charles: (*brooding*) More than I care to remember.

Louise: I'm sure that your heroes were glad to suffer in your cause.

Charles: (*snapping*) Don't be so bloody stupid, woman. Nobody in his right mind is *glad* to suffer like that.

Louise: (*sarcastically*) My apologies, Sire. For overestimating the loyalty of your subjects.

Charles: You cannot, Madam, overestimate the loyalty of men who stood in the wind and the rain on that bloody moor at Culloden, facing Cumberland's artillery.

Louise: (*exasperated*) Oh God.

Charles: Cut down like so much chaff. Many of them no more than boys. Children!

Louise: (*bored*) Yes, Sire.

Charles: Heroes, Madam. Heroes. Every one of them. Dead for a cause that was...

Louise: Lost?

Charles: I was about to say betrayed.

Louise: I'm sure His Majesty did his very best.

Charles: Which was, not, however, good enough.

Louise: I did not say that.

Charles: But that is what you meant, is it not?

Louise: (*sullenly*) I did not say that.

Charles: But you *are* saying that I failed.

Louise: (*irritably*) Well, Sire, you plainly did not succeed.

Charles: Did I not?

Louise: Or we would not be sitting here in Florence, would we?

Charles: In considerable comfort.

Louise: But being shunned by the Grand Duke and ignored by polite society.

Charles: (*coldly*) For which you blame me?

    Louise is silent. Charles is angry and growing angrier by the minute.

Charles: I said, Madam, for which you blame me? Answer me, dammit!

Louise: (*sullenly*) Who *should* I blame?

Charles: Who should you blame?

Louise: (*defiantly*) Yes. Who should I blame?

Charles: I'll tell you who you should blame. You should blame the King of France for failing – no, for refusing – to send me the soldiers and the weapons I needed for my venture. You should blame the people of Britain for failing – no, for refusing – to stand up for their rightful monarch. You should blame the Hanoverian pigs for rooting in a trough that's not their own. You should blame the bloody Popes of Rome for refusing to recognise me as the King of England. May they roast in Hell.

Louise crosses herself at this insult to the Popes.

Charles: You should blame the Grand Duke of Tuscany – and his mother the Empress – for crawling on their bellies to the Hanoverian pigs. And you should blame that wicked old sodomite Mini Mann for doing what he can to make my life – our life – a misery. That's who you should blame.

Louise: (*sullenly*) The list is long.

Charles: Aye it is. But not complete.

Louise: Is there someone else?

Charles: Aye, Madam, there is. Yourself.

Louise: (*indignantly*) Me, Sir?

Charles: Aye you, Madam. Blame yourself and your failure.

Louise: My failure?

Charles: Yes Madam, your failure. Because if *anyone* has failed in this household it is you.

Louise: How have I failed?

Charles: In the simple task for which you were selected. That is to breed.

Louise: Breed!

Charles: What else d'you think you were married for? The quality of your conversation? The brilliance of your mind? The distinction of your ancestors?

Louise: My conversation is much admired.

Charles: Aye, by horse-breakers and abortionists.

Louise: (*angrily*) And I will not have you disparage my ancestors.

Charles: (*with a sneer*) Oh you will not, will you not?

Louise: No I will not. I would remind you, Sir, that my father was Prince Gustave-Adolphe of Stolberg. And my godfather is His Royal Highness Prince Maximilian-Emanuel of Hornes. Knight of the Golden Fleece, First Class.

Charles: (*with heavy sarcasm*) Knight of the *Golden* Fleece. *First* Class. How impressive.

Louise: Sir. You must not...

Charles: Petty princelings, Madam, petty princelings. Only a fool would regard such creatures as Royal.

Louise: These petty princelings, as you call them, are of Royal blood.

Charles: Greatly diluted, I would suggest. Probably with piss.

Louise: And my father, Sire, had the decency to die in battle for *his* King. A real King.

Charles: Any fool can die in a battle. Many fools do. No, no. The fact is you were a poor choice. That is now very plain.

Louise: *I* was a poor choice?

Charles: Oh you *look* like you'd do. God knows you're young enough. You're strong enough. All the female equipment *seems* to be there.

Charles, Alfieri, Louise and Catherine

Mann, Rudd and the sleeping Charles

Louise: As it is.

Charles: Ah but the quality is not. The de Stolberg innards are not up to the task in hand. They're paltry. They're curdled. A mess of useless tripes. Fit only to produce shit. Not Kings.

Louise: (*aghast*) Sir...

Charles: Your womb, my Queen of Hearts, is not worthy of the name. It is no womb but an empty place. A desert.

Louise: My womb, Sir...

Charles: Your womb, Madam, is a blasted hollow. Nothing will ever grow there. Except, perhaps, bile. (*he spits the word out*) Bile aplenty. *Ha capi?*

> *Louise is taken aback by the ferocity of the attack. She reels then recovers.*

Louise: My womb may be empty. So far. But it is thirty years younger than that *thing* between your legs. That stump. That thing that I refuse to dignify with the name of cock.

Charles: (*smiling coldly*) Call it what you will. But unlike your womb, Madam, that stump has done its work in the past.

Louise: Hah!

Charles: And given the right receptacle, it'll do it again. Of that I'm sure.

Louise: Then you're the only one in Europe who is.

Charles: My daughter Charlotte is there for the world to see.

Louise: Oh, *Charlotte*. We're talking about Charlotte, are we? The Scotch washerwoman's brat. Your only begotten. Or misbegotten.

Charles: My daughter, Madam. And my heir.

Louise: Oh dear. The proud father! Singing the praises of the offspring he's done his best to avoid for years.

Charles: For political reasons. As you well know.

Louise: The poor little bitch has been writing you begging letters for decades. And all you've ever done is ignore them.

Charles: Have a care, Madam. A wife can go too far.

Louise: She's yours, is she? This precious little Charlotte? You're sure of that, are you?

Charles: Of course I'm sure.

Louise: How do you know?

Charles: Oh, I know. I know.

Louise: How *can* you know? When her mother was the Jacobite army's whore. The harlot of the Highlands. They say that Miss Walkinshaw fucked to the beat of a drum. Boom! Next. Boom! Next. Boom! Next...

Charles: (*shouting*) Dammit, you bitch.

Louise: (*now in full flight*) They tell me that they lined up by the *regiment* to pleasure Miss Walkinshaw.

Charles: Liar!

Louise: And your *daughter*, as you choose to call her, might just as well have been fathered by the regimental goat. Or the Duke of Cumberland.

Charles: (*shouting*) Take care, you miserable little whore.

But Louise is now consumed with hatred, and spitting like a fury. The disappointment and resentment of nine years is pouring out of her.

Louise: Perhaps if your bare-arsed Highland heroes hadn't spent so much energy pleasuring *Miss* Wilkinshaw, they might have won a few of His Majesty's battles. Instead of being chased all over Britain by *real* soldiers.

Charles: (*almost incoherent with rage*) You poisonous little...

Louise: And if they had, maybe you wouldn't be floundering in the swamps of Florence, pretending to be a King.

Charles: Damn you, damn you...

Louise: (*now beside herself with contempt*) The Great Pretender. The joke of Europe. A comic figure out of an *opera buffa*. A fat, drunken, *impotent* buffoon who should be on the other side of the lights. Wearing a cardboard crown and carrying a tinsel sceptre. The King of a paper kingdom. Your face painted and powdered – like the eunuch you are.

Charles: (*slowly, threateningly*) You evil little bitch! You sluttish monster.

With a roar Charles lunges at her. She screams and scampers out of the way; he trips and falls heavily on the floor. He groans and whimpers. He tries to rise and fails. He is like a stranded whale, wheezing and blowing. She circles him like a terrier round a fallen stag, darting in to poke him with her foot.

Louise: (*viciously*) Look at him. The King of England. The pride of Britain. The 'Bonnie Prince' of Scotland. Too bloated, feeble and fat to get to his feet.

Charles: (*almost weeping in rage*) You bitch. You miserable little...

Louise: A mockery of a man. That's what you are, *mia Carlucco*. A mockery of a man. Not enough strength to support your own belly. And with a cock that can do nothing but *dangle*.

Charles: Damn you, damn you...

Louise: (*hissing*) Well, perhaps its time that the Bonnie Prince learned a few things. Perhaps it's time that *His Majesty* learned that other, better and *younger* men have been doing his duty for him.

Charles: (*piteously*) Oh God...

Louise: Men with some gunpowder and shot in their lockers. Men whose privates are martial enough to stand to attention when a lady comes close.

Charles: Oh you little whore...

Louise: Men with the fornicating equipment to send a lady to sleep satisfied. Strong men. Lusty men. Young men. Men like Vittorio Alfieri...

In her rapture of spite she moves too close. He lunges and clutches her ankle. He pulls her down, and swarms over her, tearing and pulling at her clothes. She screams.

Charles: (*panting*) This time you'll learn. This time you'll learn. This time I'll teach you. This time...

Louise: (*screaming*) No! No! Please. No! Help me God! No! No...!

He tries to rape her. John Stewart rushes in and pulls him away.

Stewart: No, Sir. No! No!

The lights go down on the squalid scene.

Scene Six

Mann's Palazzo. Mann, Rudd and Catherine. They are grouped around the table. She has been telling her story. They are astonished.

Mann: What an extraordinary story. Can this be true?

Catherine: Yes Sir, it is true.

Mann: Surely not?

Catherine: I heard her myself. Screaming and screaming and screaming. It was terrible. Terrible! Horrible!

Mann: It must have been.

Catherine: The servants had to drag the brute away from her. He was trying to force himself on her. Ravish her. He was like some kind of wild beast.

Rudd: The bugger's mad. They should lock him up.

Catherine: She was bruised and scratched all over her body. Her arms and neck and legs and breast. I saw it when I bathed her. She cried for days. My poor Lady.

Mann: Dear, dear. And the Lady has fled, you say?

Catherine: Yes Sir. We are now living at the Convent of the White Nuns.

Rudd: On the Via del Mandorlo?

Catherine: Yes.

Mann: Will she ever go back?

Catherine: No Sir. She will not.

Mann: And the Pretender was content to let her go?

Catherine: He was not. It had to be done by subterfuge.

Mann: What kind of subterfuge?

Catherine: We arranged an outing to admire the lace and embroidery made by the White Nuns. Then, when we got to the convent, My Lady and I slipped through the gate. And it was quickly locked behind us.

Mann: And the Abbess knew of this?

Catherine: It was the Abbess who locked the gate.

Rudd: (*laughing*) Damn. Couldn't have done better myself.

Mann: What happened then?

Catherine: His Majesty – the Count I mean – banged and shouted and swore. But the Abbess would not let him into the convent. She told him that we were now under her protection. And that of the Holy Roman Church.

Rudd: Hah! That must have given the old fool an apoplexy.

Catherine: He was very upset.

Rudd: I'll wager he was.

Mann: What did he do?

Catherine: He stood outside the gate for almost an hour. Shouting through the grill, demanding to be let in. Calling over and over that he was the King of England, and must not be treated this way.

Mann: And what did the Abbess do?

Catherine: She told him to go away or she would call the town guard.

Mann: And did he go away?

Catherine: Eventually, yes. But I think he was in tears.

Mann: (*shaking his head*) Oh dear. The King of England. In tears. On the public street.

Rudd: Fool!

Mann: And now?

Catherine: Everything is arranged. My Lady and I are to go to Rome. The Count's brother the Cardinal is to give us shelter.

Rudd: You're going to live with Henry? Dear God.

Catherine: (*resentfully*) He's arranged a pension for My Lady.

Mann: (*smoothly*) Well, I'm sure that she deserves it. After *all* that she has suffered. She has paid dearly for the dregs of Royalty.

Catherine: She has.

Mann: But I'm sure that you'll find Cardinal Henry to be an excellent host.

Catherine: I hope so.

Mann: And there is no question of your mistress being in ah, well, how shall I say, a delicate condition?

Catherine: No Sir. No question of that.

Mann: Good. Good. And Count Alfieri?

Catherine: He will follow us to Rome. When the time is right.

Mann: Ah, I see. All's well that ends well, as another great dramatist once said. Well, Mademoiselle de Maltzam. It seems that your service to King George is at an end.

Catherine: Yes Sir. I think so.

Mann fishes in his desk for the final payment.

Mann: There is a little extra here, for you. Just a token of our appreciation.

Catherine: Thank you, Sir Horace.

Mann: (*with mock formality*) May I say on behalf of His Brittanic Majesty that your labours have been most valuable. King George remembers who his friends are.

Rudd: Couldn't have done it without you. That's for sure.

Mann: And, of course, Mister Rudd and I would like to offer our personal thanks. Wouldn't we Mister Rudd?

Rudd: We certainly would.

He offers his hand. She shakes it and curtsies. She shakes hands with Rudd and does not curtsy.

Catherine: Thank you, gentlemen. Thank you both. But that vile man, that so-called King (*she spits the word out*) treated My Lady so badly, so cruelly, so *disgracefully* that... Well, I am pleased to have been some assistance.

Mann: Yes. He is a wretched creature, isn't he?

Catherine: More wretched than you know, Sir. Oh, before I go, there is something...

She fishes in her purse and hands Mann a piece of paper.

Catherine: This is a passage from Count Alfieri's play about Mary Stuart. My Lady copied it. I think it might amuse you.

Mann: Thank you. We'll read it with interest.

Catherine: Good day, gentlemen. And goodbye.

Mann: Goodbye, Mademoiselle. Mister Rudd will show you out.

Rudd leaves with Catherine, and Mann settles back with the piece of paper. He reads, laughs. He shakes his head. then laughs again.

Mann: Dear, oh dear, oh dear.

Rudd returns.

Rudd: Well that's one fat Jacobite cow I'm happy to see the back of. Simpering old bitch.

Mann: (*offhandedly*) Useful though. Haters like her come cheap. Unduly fond of her mistress, I suspect. But I must say that I *do* like her parting shot at the Pretender.

Rudd: Good is it?

Mann: I'll say. Listen to this.
'O despicable race
Yea thou wilt one day see thine end.
O thou Last offshoot of it, will the sword destroy thee?
No, not a hand is vile enough to deign
To soil itself with blood like thine... '

Rudd: Not bad.

Mann: Not bad? It's masterly. And there's more.

He goes on declaiming in an actorly voice.

Mann: 'Thy life
Will pass in one long slothful sleep, while he
Who'll hold thy throne will not thy foeman be
Thy battlefield will be the table; thou
In drunken revels wilt the memory drown
Of thy unmerited, untasted reign... '

He stops and shakes his head.

Mann: Now isn't that the very *picture* of the Pretender. 'Thou in drunken revels wilt the memory drown, of thy unmerited, untasted reign... '

Rudd: Very accomplished, I'm sure. But will the world ever know *who* Alfieri was writing about?

Mann: Of course the world will. You and I, Jonathan, will make sure of that.

Rudd: Of course.

Mann: Which is only just. Count Alfieri is plainly a very great playwright. And you know how *fond* King George is of the theatre.

They laugh together.

Scene Seven

The Palazzo Guadagni. Charles is lying slumped in his chair. His bandaged leg is propped up on a footstool. There is a table at his side with a bottle on it. He is drunk, maudlin and lonely. Stewart enters.

Charles: Stewart, my man. Stewart. Come here.

Stewart: Yes Sire.

Charles: I want to confide something to you.

Stewart: Yes Sir.

Charles: (*conspiratorially*) I knew all the time. Oh yes. I knew what was going on. I could see it in her eyes, the little German slut. I knew. But I was just biding my time. Waiting, you see. Waiting to *pounce*. That's the way of it. That's what happened.

Stewart: Yes Sir.

Charles: When the time came, I sprang my trap and drove them out. By God I did! Like Saint Patrick driving the snakes out of Ireland.

Stewart: (*wearily*) Yes Sir.

Charles: And don't let anybody tell you different. I drove them out like the dogs – and the bitches – they were. With their tails between their miserable legs. And good riddance to them.

Stewart: As you say, Sir. Good riddance.

Charles: Good riddance.

> *He lapses into brooding, muttering, silence. Stewart waits patiently. He knows there is more to come.*

Charles: Tell me Stewart. How long have you been with me?

Stewart: Close on forty years.

Charles: Forty years, eh? We've seen some ups and downs in that time, you and I.

Stewart: We have that, Sir.

Charles: And d'ye like Florence? The truth now.

Stewart: I like Florence fine. (*after a pause*) But I'd rather be in Atholl.

Charles: I thought you were a Glengarry man?

Stewart: No, Sir. Atholl.

Charles: And you'd like to see Atholl again?

Stewart: I would, Sir. I would like that.

Charles: Ah well, perhaps you'll see Atholl again. Who knows? There are things that servants can do that Kings cannot.

Stewart: I'm sure that's true, Sir.

Charles: But there are some things that a King can do. And one of them is have his family around him. I've decided to send for my daughter Charlotte, you know.

Stewart: Your daughter, Sire?

Charles: Yes, Stewart. My daughter Charlotte. She'll be the new Duchess of Albany. My only heir.

Stewart: Well, I am very pleased to hear that, Sire.

Charles: Oh, yes. There'll be a new mistress at the Palazzo Guadagni. And one with good Scots blood in her veins. Good Scots blood, you see. That's what I want around me now. People of good Scots blood. People like yourself, I suppose.

Stewart: Thank you Sir. It is good of you to say so.

Charles: Not at all, Stewart. Credit where credit is due. And when she gets here, when my daughter gets here, d'ye know what I'm going to do?

Stewart: No Sir.

Charles: What I'm going to do, Stewart, what I'm going to do, is make her my *consort*. What d'ye think of that, eh?.

Stewart: I'm sure the Lady will be most pleased, Sire.

Charles: By God, that'll show that German bitch and her Eye-talian poet. By God, that'll make them squirm.

Stewart: I'm sure you're right, Sire.

Charles: By God I am. My own daughter. A Stuart of the blood. Presiding over the Palazzo Guadagni. Countess of Albany. A Knight of the Thistle. And, one day, Queen of England.

Stewart: Of course, Sire. Very good, Sire.

Charles: By God that'll make them squirm. Let them write poems about *that*!

Charles descends once more into a brooding, muttering, semi-silence.

Charles: They'll be eating their poetical hearts out, the pair of them. I'll make them a laughing stock. The joke of Europe. The butt of the civilised world. When Charlotte becomes Queen of England...

Stewart: Yes, Sire.

Charles lapses into silence.

Stewart: Will that be all, Sire?

Charles: Yes, Stewart. That will be all.

The Blasphemer

First performed by

Fifth Estate

at the

Netherbow Theatre, Edinburgh

7 November 1990

Reverend George Meldrum	Allan Sharpe
Thomas Aikenhead	Stevie Hannan
Margaret Johnstone	Gowan Calder
Mungo Craig	Gary Bakewell
Sir James Stewart of Goodtrees	Charles Kearney
Patrick Hume, Lord Polwarth	Robin Thomson
Spence	Steven McNicoll
Turnkey } Doomster }	Gordon Neish

Stage Manager	Jonathan Tait
Deputy Stage Manager	Estelle van Warmelo
Assistant Stage Manager	Owen Baldock

Director	Sandy Neilson
Designer	Paul Ambrose Wright
Lighting Design	John Cassidy
Costume Design	Hania Dzikowska
Scenic Artist	Mike McLoughlin
Production Manager	Sean Miller

The Blasphemer

Dramatis Personae

George Meldrum: One of the two ministers at the Tron Kirk in Edinburgh and a major participant in the tragedy of Thomas Aikenhead. He was Moderator of the General Assembly in 1698 (the year after Aikenhead's death) and again in 1703. He was made Professor of Divinity at Edinburgh in 1701. The son of an Aberdeen merchant, Meldrum was 'deprived' of his living in Aberdeen in 1662 by the Bishops, then restored to it when he changed his mind and took an oath of allegiance to the Episcopacy. In 1688 he was 'translated' to Kilwinning, and 1692 to the Tron Kirk in Edinburgh. Unmarried, he was described as a kindly but excessively pious man. When Thomas Aikenhead was thrown in the Tolbooth for blasphemy (almost certainly at Meldrum's instigation) his most regular visitor was George Meldrum. He pleaded with the Privy Council for a stay of execution. In later years he wrote pamphlets defending the "splendour and beauty of the office of informer..." His dying words (of which there are two versions) repeated over and over, were "Worthy is the Lamb that was slain..."

Thomas Aikenhead: A student at Edinburgh University, either of medicine or divinity: the record is not clear. The son of a mildly notorious quack surgeon who had been hauled before the Privy Council for selling bogus aphrodisiacs, Aikenhead was a scholarly youth who became caught up in the 'advanced' theo-philosophy of his day, particularly with the 'Deistic' philosophers such as Thomas Hobbes, Lord Herbert of Cherbury and John Toland. His opinions got back to the authorities – almost certainly via George Meldrum – and he was indicted, tried and executed for blasphemy. He was hanged on January 8th 1697 at the Gallowlea in Edinburgh. In his gallows speech he claimed to be a faithful Christian and died with a bible in his hands.

Patrick Hume, Lord Polwarth: The Lord Chancellor of the Privy Council at the time of Aikenhead's trial and execution, who used his casting vote in favour of the death sentence. A hard-line Protestant and fanatical anti-Jacobite, Hume was a border laird who was in and out of Scottish jails in the days of the Stuarts, and who was mixed up in both the Rye plot to assassinate James VII, and the Duke of Argyll's abortive invasion of Scotland in 1685. He fled to the continent where he posed as a Scottish doctor, and returned to Britain with William of Orange in 1688. In 1689 he became MP for Berwickshire, was made Lord Polwarth in 1690, and in May 1696, became Lord Chancellor of the Privy Council, the most powerful man in Scotland. He was known (and feared) for his disdain of everyone whose zeal for the Protestant cause was less than his. In 1697 he was made Earl of Marchmont and in 1702 became the High Commisoner to the General Assembly of the Church of Scotland.

Sir James Stewart of Goodtrees: An accomplished lawyer whose father had been the Lord Provost of Edinburgh. Known as something of an ambitious trimmer, Stewart had switched allegiance between the Jacobites and Whigs a number of times. He ended up on the right side and returned to Scotland with William of Orange. He was the King's Lord Advocate in Scotland from 1692 to 1709 and from 1711 to 1713, a close friend and something of an admirer of Patrick Hume, Lord Polwarth. Stewart is said to have been rescued from death's door in 1700 by the prayers of George Meldrum.

Margaret Johnstone: Aikenhead's sweetheart, aged 16. A fictional character.

Mungo Craig: One of Thomas Aikenhead's like-minded fellow students, it seems that it was Craig who introduced Aikenhead to the Deistic writers by lending him books. Craig appears to have been 'turned' by the authorities, and he wrote a wicked little pamphlet calling for Aikenhead's death, which was published before the trial (there is some suggestion that it may have been drafted by the authorities). Craig then gave evidence for the prosecution. According to John Locke, who studied the trial, his evidence was crucial. He was the only witness to swear that Aikenhead had actually 'railed against Christ' in terms of the Act under which he was executed. He wrote another pamphlet *after* the execution denying the charges made against him in Aikenhead's gallows speech. There is no record of what happened to Craig after the trial and execution of Aikenhead. He probably flourished.

Act I

Scene One

The minister's study. An elderly minister, dressed in clerical grey and wearing a white choker, is seated at a table, scribbling, reading, and muttering to himself. The table is covered with papers and books, as are the chairs and some of the floor. He stands up and begins to rummage through them in an irritated kind of way.

Meldrum: Look at this place. Look at it. Wad ye credit the state o this room. Whit kind o wey is this for a grown man tae live? Dammit whaur is everythin? Margaret! Margaret Johnstone! Where are ye woman? Wid ye come in here...

He continues to search around among the papers, grumbling to himself. He gets up and walks round the table.

Meldrum: Ach, I should hae married. I should hae found masel a wife, instead o livin here masel like some bluidy Popish priest. Wi a young woman tae look efter me that canna stand the sicht o me. A meenister needs a wife, jist like onie ither man. And a meenister needs bairns, jist like onie ither man. Ye can learn frae bairns.

He stops rummaging and stares into the middle distance

Meldrum: For ane thing ye can learn tae tell a bairn's daftness frae a bairn's wickedness.

He sighs, shrugs, and resumes his search.

Meldrum: Dammit, dammit. I'm gettin auld. I've half forgotten whit it is I'm lukkin for. If she'd jist leave things alane, I'd be able tae find whit I'm, lukkin for... Margaret! Where is the wumman? Paper, paper, paper...

He stops and reflects.

Meldrum: I kent a man once wha was killed by paper. He was hunted doon in a *labyrinth* o paper – indictments and judgements, pamphlets and complaints, letters and petitions, acts o assembly and acts o parliament. Even holy texts. Bits and pieces o paper. But they crushed the life oot o him. Aye did they!

He finds a document and plucks it out of the debris, almost triumphantly.

Meldrum: Here it is! I wrote this, oh, in the year of Our Lord 1701. Fower year efter the events at Golgotha on the walk tae Leith. I titled it (*he quotes*) "A private Letter Asserting the Lawfulness of Informing Against the Vicious and Profane Before the Courts of Immorality..." A resoundin title, ye'll hae tae agree. A lot o fowk read it. A lot o fowk *commented* on it. Ay... they commented on it aa richt.

Whit it was, ye see, wis a wee pamphlet on the *necessitie* – ay that's the only ward for it – on the necessitie of informin on blasphemers, and idolators and other sic Godless fowk. By giein their names and tellin their crimes tae His Majesty's law officers.

Some o my friens hae asked me why I never pit my name tae it. They thocht it odd that I should publish sic an *upliftin* piece o work anoniemouslie. And I usually tell them that it's just no *dignified* for a meenister at the Tron Kirk in Edinburgh tae be pittin his name tae the public prints.

Ither fowk say I'm just bein canny. And wha's tae blame me for that? The thing is, nae matter hou Godly and righteous the cause... naebody likes an informer. But we need them. Oh, we need them aa richt. Ye see, whit I canna get fowk tae understaun is that if ye let blasphemy, and idolatry and Godlessness run riot in a land, then ye're riskin the wrath o God. Ye're in danger o ... where is it... ? Oh ay...

He reads again

Meldrum: "... pulling down the direful vengeance of an offended God upon a poor distressed land... "

Sae! Tae *alloo* the blasphemers tae go unchecked is a kind o *treason.* That's whit it is. It's a crime against your country, as weel as a crime against the souls o your fellow men. Sae it follows that every man and woman in Scotland has a *patriotic* duty to inform on blasphemers. D'ye see that? Eh? Therefore it follows that...

He reads again

Meldrum: "... to inform against the immoral and vicious is honourable, equitable and charitable... "

He stops and replaces the pamphlet on the table.

Meldrum: Ay. Honourable, equitable and charitable. Braw wards. Wards that fair roll oot yer mooth. But did they stop the gabbin o the Edinburgh gossips? Did they bring an end tae the sniggerin? They did not. I'll aye be *that* meenister. Till the end o my days – which micht no be lang noo – I'll be Meldrum the informer. The treacherous auld *clype!*

He stops, and resumes his seat at the table.

Meldrum: They're wrang o coorse. I'm no a *bad* man. Or a wicked man. Wad the Lord hae allooed a *wicked* man tae reach sic eminence in his Kirk o Scotland? Naa, naa, the Lord is on my side. I'm as shair o that as I'm shair o the fact that there is...

He recites ponderously

Meldrum: "... a splendour and beauty to the office of an informer... "

He breaks off distractedly

Meldrum: But that splendour and beauty that I wrote aboot didna mak me popular wi the fowk o Edinburgh. But it micht hae been easier tae thole if I'd had a family. Sometimes, in my weakness I see him as the son I never had. The son I *should* hae had. A fine, bricht, mettlesome lad wi nimble wits and a strong mind. As the Lord kens, I begin tae weary. My steps are falterin. I could dae wi the steadyin hand o a guid strang son...

He broods some more. Then, quite suddenly he straightens up, climbs to his feet and sheds a dozen years. He dons wig, coat, muffler and hat. He begins to rub his hands together vigorously as if cold.

Meldrum: It was, oh, mair nor twal years syne. On a cauld October nicht in the year of Our Lord 1696. I had jist locked the door o the Kirk behind me tae walk doon the High Street tae my manse. I was weary and cauld. An auld man, vexed and irritated by his day. Lukkin forrit tae naethin mair nor his supper, and a cup o brandy wine in front o a guid fire...

Scene Two

As Meldrum descends the steps of the Tron Kirk he encounters three young people, two men and a girl. The men might be slightly drunk. They are in high spirits and quite noisy, but good-natured. The girl is linked into both men. They are Margaret Johnstone, her sweetheart Thomas Aikenhead, and his friend and fellow student, Mungo Craig.

Margaret: A cauld nicht, Maister Meldrum, a cauld nicht.

Meldrum: (*startled out of his thoughts*) Oh! Ay, that it is. A sair cauld nicht. Guid evenin tae ye Margaret. And tae ye gentlemen.

Craig: Guid evenin, meenister.

Aikenhead: Guid evenin, Sir.

Meldrum: Whit brings three young fowk oot on a nicht like this?

Craig: Jist takin oor pleasure, Sir.

Meldrum: o the seemly sort, I trust?

Craig: O coorse.

Meldrum: No that ye'd tell me if it was the other kind, eh?

Margaret: I'll mak shair that these twa callants dinna stray aff the path, meenister.

Meldrum: And richt pleased I am tae hear it. No that I'd be ower *censorious* o a cup o heated brandy wine on a nicht like this.

Aikenhead: (*laughing*) The kind o nicht when a spark oot o Hell wid no go amiss.

Meldrum: (*surprised*) A spark oot o Hell, Sir?

Aikenhead: The cauld, meenister, the cauld. We could dae wi a few o the flames o Hellfire on a nicht like this. Tae warm oor fingers ower. No that I'd be expectin to find the flames o Hellfire on the steps o the Tron Kirk.

Meldrum: (*laughing*) I should hope no, young gentleman. But I fear I maun tak issue wi ye there. There's a puckle mair tae Hellfire nor twa handfus o warm fingers. Foreby, it's the cauldest place imaginable.

Craig: Cauld, meenister?

Meldrum: Aye cauld. Whit could be caulder nor a place where God's love doesna reach?

Craig: (*laughing*) A queer place yon Hell then. Where a body will raist an freeze at yin and the same time.

Meldrum: Oh, I've nae doot it's queer. Queer and terrible ayont oor imaginins.

He laughs again, and makes to go.

Meldrum: But this is nae time or place tae be debatin Hell and Hellfire wi three braw young fowk. Awa tae yer, eh, seemly pleasures. I'm awa tae my supper.

Aikenhead: But that canna be richt.

Meldrum: Whit canna be richt, Sir? That a hungry auld meenister needs his supper?

Aikenhead: Naa, naa. Whit ye said aboot Hell bein ayont oor imaginins. It seems tae me that Hell has been weel imagined. Ower and ower again.

Matthew eleven and sixteen. Luke twenty-six. Saint Paul's letter tae the Corinthians, twenty-five. The Revelation o Saint John one, six and twenty.

Meldrum: (*indulgently*) And ye've missed oot Matthew Five, ten, thirteen, eighteen and twenty-three. As weel as James three and the second book of Peter chapter two.

Meldrum laughs, but is interested.

Meldrum: Sae! A young gentleman wi a *speculative* turn o mind. Weel, I tak yer point Maister... eh...

Aikenhead: Aikenhead, meenister. Thomas Aikenhead. And this is ma frien Mungo Craig. Baith o us students at the toun's college.

They shake hands.

Margaret: (*proudly*) Tammas is my sweetheart, Sir. And has been fower months syne. We're hopin tae be mairrit.

Which remark is met with a resentful glare from Mungo Craig.

Meldrum: Weel I'm shair ye'll hae my blessings on it when the time comes, Margaret. (*he catches Craig's eye*) If no Maister Craig's. I tak yer point Maister Aikenhead. But I fear ye miss mine.

Aikenhead: And whit point is that, meenister?

Meldrum: Sic accoonts o Hell that we hae come frae the holy scripture. And that, as ye maun ken, was no written oot o the imaginins o men, but by minds filled wi the ward o God. Which tells us that Hell is a maist fearfu and dreadfu place.

Aikenhead: Jist the thing tae fricht puir bodies.

Margaret: Wheesht Tammas. Dinna start yon nonsense. Let the meenister awa tae his supper.

Meldrum: Ay, that's ane idea the meenister wad heartily welcome. My auld feet are beginnin tae feel like bits o ice. I ken Mistress Johnstone here fine, but wha's flock are ye gentlemen frae?

Craig: Ah...

Aikenhead: Nae man's flock, Sir.

Meldrum: Ah, me. Ah, me. Twa sheep withoot a shepherd. Wanderin the hillside in winter. Are ye no feart o the wolves?

Craig: (*laughing*) There's no ower monie left in the streets o Edinburgh meenister.

Meldrum: Ah, but there ye're wrang young man. They're lurkin in every doorwey and up every close. Just waitin tae rend your immortal soul. Weel Maister Craig, ye and yer frien here are aye welcome tae shelter in the fold o the Tron Kirk. Should the wilderness ever become ower muckle for ye.

Aikenhead: There's some o us that dinna see it as a wilderness, meenister. Just a fine open space where we can run, and breathe and think fine thochts.

Craig: And no be trochled by ower-anxious shepherds. Eh Tammas?

Aikenhead: Ay. Ye micht say that.

Margaret is beginning to fret at the drift of the conversation. She senses danger.

Margaret: Wheesht Tammas. Never listen tae him, Maister Meldrum. His heid is full o havers and book-learnin. Come awa, Tammas, before the meenister taks offence at yer spielin.

Craig: Ay Tammas...

Meldrum: (*coldly*) Is that hou ye see us, gentlemen. As men whae trochle free spirits like yersel?

Craig is startled by the minister's chilly response.

Craig: No that...

Aikenhead: Nae personal offence intended, meenister. I'm speakin in the generality o things noo.

Meldrum: And are there monie o ye in Scotland that think as ye dae?

Aikenhead: Mair nor ye micht think, meenister.

Meldrum: Ye wid be surprised at hou muckle I fear the spread o Godlessness, Sir.

Margaret: We'll be sayin guid nicht tae ye noo Sir... Tammas...

Meldrum: And does the Guid Book, the Holy Ward o the Lord, mean naethin tae ye?

Aikenhead: It means mair tae me nor ye wid credit. But it disna mean *everythin*. I like tae find meanin in the warks o aa the fowk that try tae find an answer tae this warld's riddles.

Meldrum: And wha wid these fowk be?

Aikenhead: Weel... there is the Greek philosophers. Aristotle and Epicurus.

Meldrum: Pagan Tosh!

Aikenhead: Monsieur Descartes. The Dutchman Grotius. Baruch Spinoza...

Meldrum: A Jew, unless I'm mistaken.

Aikenhead: And Englishmen, Sir. Men frae oor ain island. Like Thomas Hobbes, John Locke, Herbert of Cherbury. The Irishman John Toland...

Meldrum: Ah! The celebrated Maister Toland. I was wonderin if that name wid be mentioned.

Aikenhead: A keen intellect, Sir.

Meldrum: A Papist renegade, Sir. A disgrace tae Glasgow University. A man wha's book has jist been *burned,* consigned to the fire by the public hangman in Ireland.

Aikenhead: The mair shame on Ireland.

Meldrum: (*angry now*) The mair shame on *ye* young man for entertainin the ideas o sic a man.

Aikenhead: I maun disagree wi ye, Sir. Maister Toland is a man o maist eminent sense.

Meldrum: Thank God the courts o Ireland tak anither view.

Aikenhead: Naa, Sir. They are wrang. And Maister Toland is richt tae state that the name o religion is abused by ambition, impiety and contention.

Meldrum: (*sarcastically*) Noo there's an original thocht. Martin Luther, ye micht never hae lived. Ye dare quote your paltry script at me? Weel alloo me to quote mine at *ye*. Saint Paul's letter tae the Galatians, chapter one, verse eight. "But though ye, or an angel frae heaven, preach onie other gospel unto ye nor that which we hae preached unto ye, *let him be accursed...*"

Aikenhead: Accursed...? For usin the brain and the tongue that I was born wi?

Meldrum: The tongue, Maister Aikenhead, is a fell dangerous instrument. As is written in the book o James "But the tongue can no man tame, it is an unruly evil, full of deadly poison..."

Before Aikenhead can reply Meldrum rounds on Mungo Craig, who is looking anxious.

Meldrum: And ye, Maister Craig. Do ye share Maister Aikenhead's *enthusiasm* for the works o Maister Hobbes, Maister John Toland and the rest o that *atheistical* crew?

Craig: (*confused and embarrassed*) Me, Sir? Some o them. Not aa. Maister Aikenhead and I hae had our disagreements. But, I... ah...

Aikenhead: Maister Craig is a man wha hasna yet made up his mind. No in public oniewey.

Meldrum: But ye *hae* made up your mind I tak it? Tae reject the redemption o your soul through the Lord Jesus Christ. Are ye seekin the very Hell that seems tae *interest* ye sae muckle.

Aikenhead: Whit I'm *seekin*, meenister, is a better warld nor this.

Meldrum: And in yer pursuit o that *better warld* ye maun deny yer God.

Aikenhead: There ye hae me wrang, meenister. I'm no denyin my God. I believe that the Lord created aathin we can and canna see. Every star, muin and comet in the heavens. Every grain o sand and every creepin thing on this earth, oorsels included.

Meldrum: As we are telt by the Holy Scripture.

Aikenhead: As ye say. But...

Meldrum: I kent there wid be a but.

Aikenhead: ...But it seems tae me that God has sae ordered things that nae angel, or archangel, or messiah, or prophet or holy saviour is aboot tae step doon oot o heaven and save us. We maun dae that for oorsels.

Meldrum: I see. God the absentee laird. God the errant faither wha brings his bairns intae the warld and then abandons them.

Aikenhead: Ay weel...

Meldrum: Like some drunken sot oot o the Coogate. Is that your idea o the Lord?

Aikenhead: Better that, shairlie, nor tae see Him as *wilfully* inflictin sic evil on his bairns. Whae's the better faither? My God whae abandons us tae struggle wi disease and famine and cruelty as best we can? Or your God whae *persecutes* us wi those self-same evils?

Meldrum: (*becoming more and angry*) Whit ye are proposin, Sir, is God as the lesser o twa evils. As wicked a theology as ever I heard.

Meldrum: Hou else d'ye accoont for pain, disease and war?

Meldrum: (*ignoring him*) And whaur's the place in this, ah, scheme o things for the Lord Jesus Christ and his ineffable love?

Aikenhead: I fear there's nae place for him. Except as ane o a wheen o prophets and great men o religion. Like Moses, and Mohammed, and the Buddha o the Indian fowk.

Meldrum: Whit sad trash!

Margaret: (*desperately*) Ye'll hae to forgie him, Maister Meldrum. He's been in wan howff ower monie. His pate is addled wi ower muckle wine. He's jist rantin on, shawin aff.

Meldrum: (*shaking his head*) I fear there is mair tae it nor that.

Margaret: Naa! Pey him nae heed. He's jist a daft laddie. That's whit ye are, Tammas Aikenhead. A daft laddie. I want tae gang hame noo, Tammas...

Aikenhead: Ay, richt Margaret.

Meldrum: (*ignoring her pleas*) Correct me if I'm wrang, Maister Aikenhead, but are ye no describin that theology which is now called *Deism*?

Aikenhead: Some cry it Deism, meenister. Masel I see it as the licht o reason.

Meldrum: And *I* see it as a stagin post on the road to Godless atheism. And dae ye and your friend here describe yersels as Deists?

Craig: I widna say that, meenister. I'm no shair aboot that...

Aikenhead: Maister Craig maun speak for himsel. I just see masel as yaisin my ain wits, me, tae try tae find my ain answers. I can see naethin wrang wi that.

Meldrum: Weel I can, young man, I can.

Aikenhead: (*shrugging*) As ye will, Maister Meldrum.

Meldrum: Ye are a dangerous man, young Maister Aikenhead. I fear ye micht be spreadin a *contagion* in the very heart o Scotland. A threat tae yer ain and ither fowk's immortal souls.

Aikenhead: When ye talk aboot immortal souls, ye are talkin aboot somethin that naebody has seen, or heard, or felt, or smelled. In a ward, ye're talkin aboot somethin no susceptible tae human reason.

Meldrum: Reason?

Aikenhead: Ay, *reason*, meenister, reason.

Meldrum: Pshaw!

Aikenhead: No, Sir. No. Reason is the road tae the better warld for us aa. Human reason and human imagination. Twa tracks on the road tae a better future for aabody. And when they join... we'll be able tae dae oniethin... Oniethin... We'll create wonders.

Meldrum: (*contemptuously*) Wonders!

Aikenhead: Ay, wonders. Miracles the like o which were never dreamed o by your prophet Jesus Christ.

Meldrum: Tak a care, Sir. I'll no hear my God traduced at the door o my ain Kirk.

Aikenhead: I'm no talkin aboot God, Sir. I'm talkin aboot the *man* ye caa Jesus.

Meldrum: Wha is God's only begotten son. As ye ken weel.

Aikenhead: Then why is God sae *touchy* aboot his bairn? Why is he sae quick tae tak offence at oniebody wha lauchs at his laddie?

Meldrum: He'll no be mocked.

Aikenhead: Mebbe he's feart that we'll see through His loon's tricks.

Meldrum: Tricks, Sir...?

Aikenhead: Does it no seem passin strange tae ye that yer Jesus choose his followers oot o the maist sempil o fowk? Why did he no enlist some scribes, or some pharisees, or some men o learnin?

Margaret: Tammas! I'll no hae my saviour spoken aboot like yon. It's no richt.

Aikenhead: (*ignoring her and warming to his subject*) Could it be that yer saviour was *feart*?

Meldrum: The Lord? Feart?

Aikenhead: Ay. Feart that oniebody wi a modicum o sense and learnin in his heid wid see through his daft-like wizardry? I mean, whaurs the... *holiness*, in turnin jugs o watter intae wine.

Margaret: (*wailing*) Tammas...

Aikenhead: (*laughing*) A popular kind o trick I grant ye. But wha wid it impress but sots and drunkards? It's pointless.

Meldrum: I warn ye, Sir...

Aikenhead: Just aboot as pointless as walkin aboot on the tap o the sea? Whaur's the sense in *that* can ye tell me? Egyptian wizardry, tae beguile puir block-heidit countrie fowk.

Meldrum: (*shaking his head*) Tricks and wizardry is it? Is that hou ye wid describe the wondrous *cures* that oor Lord wrocht? Gaurin the blind tae see and the crippled tae walk? And the raisin o Lazarus frae amang the deid?

Aikenhead: I'd describe thae as stories pit aboot efter he was deid himsel. Fables tae mak bairns and auld women wonder. Stories that will nae stand twa seconds under the licht o reason. They micht hae worked seventeen hunner years syne, but I doot that they'll work muckle langer.

Meldrum: And will this *reason* that ye speak o replace Christ's love? Will this *imagination* o yours offer us eternal life?

Aikenhead: Maybe no. But they will mak the misery that ye see aboot ye a thing o the past. When reason has replaced yer faith, then maybe every bairn in the land will hae eneuch tae eat. We'll extirpate disease. We'll soond the death-knell o death itsel.

Meldrum: Whit trashy stuff!

Aikenhead: Naa, ye're wrang. Wi reason and imagination there is naethin we canna dae. We'll dae sic things as build *engines* that will fly through air wi mair ease nor ships sail through water. We'll hae commerce wi the warld on the muin. We'll gang tae the stars, meenister.

Meldrum: Sad trash! Sad trash!

Aikenhead: Naa, meenister. We'll mak another warld. And it'll be a better warld nor this.

Meldrum: And will there be a place in this *better warld* o yours for my Lord, Jesus Christ? And for us, the fowk wha love him?

Meldrum, Margaret, Turnkey and Aikenhead

Aikenhead: Maybe! Maybe no! That remains tae be seen. Fowk will hae tae mak up their ain minds. God kens they've been listenin tae ye preachin it at them lang eneuch.

Meldrum: The Lord's ward, Sir, the Lord's ward.

Aikenhead: Tae ye, ay. But tae me it's naethin but a rhapsody o feigned and ill-invented nonsense.

Meldrum: (*Angrily*) What?

Aikenhead: I said, Sir, that tae *me* yer Christian faith is naethin but a rhapsody o feigned and ill-invented nonsense.

Margaret: Tammas Aikenhead! Will ye stop that.

Craig: Tammas man. Ye're gaen ower faur. Haud yer wheesht...

Margaret: Maister Meldrum, ye'll hae to forgie him. He's no...

Meldrum: (*coldly*) Naa, naa. Let the young *gentleman* continue. Let's hear the rest o this philosophy.

Aikenhead: And my ain view – and it's nae mair nor that – is that yer Christianity will no last muckle efter the year 1800. Efter that, weel, your Christian religion will be replaced by somethin... mair sensible.

Meldrum: Deism nae doot.

Aikenhead: Or somethin like.

    There is a long cold pause

Meldrum: Ye realise, Maister Aikenhead, that this very year the General Assembly o the Kirk passed an Act – an Act nae less – warnin every meenister and elder in the land tae guard against this pernicious nonsense ye caa Deism. And, my God, I can see noo why that Act was thocht necessary.

Aikenhead: I mind the act.

Meldrum: And this gies ye nae pause?

Aikenhead: Should it, Sir?

Meldrum: I think it should, Sir. For that same act o the General Assembly bid aa God's people in Scotland tae fecht yer Deism wi *every weapon* at oor hands. Every weapon, Maister Aikenhead. And the Kirk has weapons that micht surprise ye. Sae here's a question for ye. And I ask ye tae weigh yer answer carefully...

Aikenhead: (*troubled now by the menace in Meldrum's voice*) Gae on.

Meldrum: The question is – am I tae tak ye seriously?

Aikenhead: Sir?

Meldrum: Am I tae tak ye seriously? Or am I tae regaird ye as a prattlin bairn? As your sweetheart here seems tae feel ye are.

Margaret: That's jist what he is, meenister. That's *aa* he is. Ye can see for yersel. Jist twenty years auld, and spoutin on like a... I dinna ken whit. I jist dinna ken whit. The best thing is tae ignore him. That's whit I dae. That's the best thing

Aikenhead: Ye canna fricht me wi yer threats o the fiery lake o Hell, meenister. Or Gehenna, or Hades, or whitever ye like tae cry it. Ye can only fricht fowk wha believe sic a place exists.

Margaret: (*wailing*) Tammas! Will ye stop speakin like yon. O coorse it *exists*. Please...?

Meldrum: I'm no talkin about the fires o Hell, laddie, I'm talkin aboot *the law o Scotland.*

Aikenhead: The law?

Meldrum: Ay, Sir. The law. Micht I remind ye that there is already a young man o yer ain age sittin in misery in the Auld Tolbooth. For speakin much the same kind o blasphemy.

Aikenhead: Ay, John Frazer. The merchant's prentis. I've never met the man but I ken aboot him. Weel, his body micht be under lock and key, but his thochts are free.

Meldrum: Ye micht find that gey little consolation, Maister Aikenhead. Gin ye ever find yersel keepin Maister Frazer company.

Aikenhead: Some things just hae tae be tholed.

Meldrum: Sae! I repeat my question. Am I tae tak ye seriously? Or am I tae receive an apology fae ye for the abuse and calumny that ye've heaped on my Lord and Saviour. Wha's yours as weel if ye but kent it.

Aikenhead: Ye'll get nae apology frae me, meenister.

Margaret: (*now thoroughly frightened*) Come on Tammas. Tell Maister Meldrum yer sorry for whit ye said. Tell him it was aa a nonsense – which it wis. Tell him that ye're sorry.

Aikenhead: I'll no apologise.

Margaret: Maister Meldrum, I'll apologise for him. Will that dae...?

Meldrum: No Margaret. I fear that'll no dae. Onie apology will hae tae come frae Maister Aikenhead himsel.

Aikenhead: Ye'll get nae apology frae me.

Margaret: Tammas...!

Meldrum is now thoroughly angered by Aikenhead's intransigence.

Meldrum: For the last time, laddie, will ye repent o yer utterances, and apologise for this *blasphemy* o yours.

Craig: Tammas. I think this has gone ower faur. Maybe ye'd better say a ward or twa o apology. Nae hairm in that. I think it's time tae...

Aikenhead: Awa an haud yer tongue, Mungo.

Margaret: Tammas!

Aikenhead: Maister Meldrum, I've nae doot yer a man that means tae dae richt. But I canna apologise tae ye withoot denyin whit I believe. Can ye no see that?

Meldrum: (*curtly and coldly*) What I *can* see is a hard-hearted and determined young blasphemer. A conceited sprig o a pedant.

Aikenhead: No, Sir.

Meldrum: Ay, Sir! Very weel, On yer ain heid be it. Ye'll be hearin mair o this.

Margaret: Maister Meldrum... please... Ye're no tae gang tae the magistrates aboot Tammas... Please. He disna ken...

Meldrum: Naa, naa Margaret. Yer young man has gone ower far. Awa wi ye. Awa wi ye. Go on! Oot o ma sicht...

The trio of young people exit, looking embarrassed and troubled. Meldrum glares after them for some time, then turns and walks to the front of the stage.

Meldrum: And here I maun admit tae the Lord, and beg his forgiveness, for the sin o anger. I admit it freely. Oh I was angry. That young man had mocked me, and vexed me and puzzled me. Him and his Deism and his talk o Hobbes and John Toland and the Jew Spinoza. And his notions about extirpatin disease... and engines that fly tae the warld in the muin. Here was I, a man o 62 years, meenister at the Tron Kirk shamed by a laddie. And on the steps o my ain Kirk. And in front o a quean frae my ain congregation. The thing was *intolerable*.

Sae, the very next morning, and wi young Maister Aikenhead's voice still ringin in my lugs, I paid a visit tae Sir James Stewart o Gutters, His Majesty's Advocate in Scotland.

Scene Three

The Advocate's house in the High Street. He is Sir James Stewart, a handsome but coarse-featured and grossly obese man in his late 50s. He cannot move without great exertion. He is often breathless. His middle-aged clerk, Thomas Spence, a spare man dressed in black, shows Meldrum in. the Advocate waves him into a chair.

Stewart: Maister Meldrum. Guid day tae ye. Sit ye doon. Can Spence here fetch ye a cup o somethin? It's a nippit kind o mornin.

Meldrum: Ye're kind, Sir James. But no thank ye.

Stewart: But ye'll no mind if I indulge myself wi some warmed up Bordeaux wine? Spence... if ye please.

Spence leaves the room.

Stewart: Noo then. What is it I can do for the meenister at the Tron Kirk?

Meldrum: *Ane* o the meenisters at the Tron Kirk.

Stewart: Oh ay. Maister Crichton is yer, eh, accomplice is he no?

Meldrum: Ay, that's richt. William Crichton. A maist godly man.

Stewart: Nae doot, nae doot.

Spence returns with the glass of mulled claret, puts it on the table in front of the Advocate and leaves the room.

Stewart: Noo, Maister Meldrum. Whit brings *ane* o the meenisters frae the Tron Kirk tae this side o the High Street.

Meldrum: Ye see before ye a man wha's heart is still stoundin in his kist wi fricht.

Stewart: Fricht, ye say?

Meldrum: Ay. Fricht. Because last nicht, on the steps o my ain Kirk, I cam face to face wi the demon o Godlessness.

Stewart is obviously unimpressed. He looks bored, with the air of a man who has heard all this before.

Stewart: Indeed?

Meldrum: Indeed.

Stewart: And whit *form* did this, ah, demon tak, if I micht ask?

Meldrum: A student, Sir. A student at the University of Edinburgh. A laddie by the name o Thomas Aikenhead. Nae mair nor 20, I wad say. A handsome eneuch loon wi a ready wit, a shairp tongue, and mair nor a smatterin o book learnin.

Stewart: There's monie sic laddies gang through the gates o the toun's college every weekday mornin, Maister Meldrum.

Meldrum: I hope not, Sir James. For if that's true then I fear for Scotland.

Stewart: He was as bad as that, eh? I presume frae what ye say that this Maister...?

Meldrum: Aikenhead. Thomas Aikenhead.

Stewart: Ay. That this Maister Thomas Aikenhead had a few wards to say against yer Kirk. Whit was he? Some kind of *Episcopalian?* Or Papist, although there seem to be damn few o them left?

Meldrum: No against my Kirk, Advocate, but against my Saviour. *Our* Saviour. The Blessed Lord, Jesus Christ.

Stewart: (*mildly interested now*) Ah... A blasphemer?

Meldrum: Ay. A blasphemer. O the worst kind. A clever, wheedlin, sneerin kind o blasphemer. Aye ready wi a joke and a mockin ward. The kind that is the darlin o his fellows. The kind that can recite the Scripture chapter and verse, and in daein it reduce it tae a mockery. But... a persuasive young man, Sir James. A *very* persuasive young man.

Stewart: Weel, I can certainly see that he vexed ye, Maister Meldrum. Did he prick yer vanity?

Meldrum: (*bridling*) Ye dae me an injustice, Sir James.

Stewart: Hou sae, Sir?

Meldrum: I'll no deny that he vexed me. But it's no on *that* accoont that I'm here. I maun insist on that.

Stewart: Ower monie fowk sit in that self same chair and tell me a wheen o lees. And, I should tell ye, some o them are clergymen.

Meldrum: I'm sorry tae hear that.

Stewart: Ay weel... Sae whit did he *say* tae ye, this Thomas Aikenhead?

Meldrum: What did he say? He questioned the existence o oor immortal souls. He belittled the miracles o Oor Lord. He ranted aboot the superiority o reason ower faith. He ranked Jesus Christ alang wi a puckle ither prophets like Moses, Mohammed and Buddha.

Stewart: Did he sae?

Meldrum: And he described my faith – oor faith – as "a rhapsody o feigned and ill-invented nonsense'. These were the very wards he used tae my face.

Stewart: Were there onie witnesses?

Meldrum: Ay. His sweetheart, Miss Margaret Johnstone – a decent eneuch quean and ane o my ain flock. And his frien, a Maister Craig. Mungo Craig I think his name was. Anither student at the university.

Stewart: Twa witnesses. Ane o them his sweetheart. Hmmm...

Meldrum: Sae! Can ye pursue this Deistical whelp afore he infects mair o the student body?

Stewart: Weel, if whit ye say is true – and I'm no dootin yer ward for a minute – I micht be able tae indict him for blasphemy or profanity.

Meldrum: That wid seem meet.

Stewart: Maybe sae. But ane man's blasphemy can be another man's, eh, philosophy.

Meldrum: There was nae doot aboot this young man's blasphemy. I can assure ye o that.

Stewart: Ay, mebbe. But witnesses can be easily confused and perplexed by a clever advocate. If we can *find* onie witnesses, that is.

Meldrum: I'd be happy tae testify.

Stewart: Ay, I'm shair that ye wid. But, wi respect tae ye, I'm no shair a jury wid regaird ye as bein 'withoot malice, prejudice and partial council', as we say at the assize. They micht see ye as a man wi, weel, a strang point o view.

Meldrum: I can see that ye're sweir.

Stewart: I am, Sir.

Meldrum: Sir James. This Protestant realm o Scotland exists by God's grace. Tae offend God is tae threaten oor land. Rampant blasphemy and apostasy could bring doon His wrath on oor ain heids. Sic blasphemy, Sir, is a kind o *treason*. There's nae ither word for it.

Stewart: I follow the argument. But I'm still sweir.

Meldrum: Then let me remind ye o the law, Sir James. The Act of 1690, passed in the May month o that year, that ratified the Westminster Confession o Faith.

Stewart: (*coldly*) I need nae remindin o the law Sir.

Meldrum: Maybe sae. But it seems ye dae need remindin o the Confession o Faith itsel. Mair particularly chapter twenty. Which states that the maintainin o erroneous opinions "... contrary to the known principles of Christianity... may lawfully be called to accoont and proceeded against by the censures o the church and *by the power of the civil magistrate ...* " That is by fowk like yersel, Sir James.

Stewart: I see ye've been at yer books. But I'm familiar wi the Confession o Faith.

Meldrum: Then if ye are, ye canna plead ignorance when I preach this Sabbath on the *failure* o His Majesty's Advocate tae respect it.

Stewart: (*after some thought*) Ye mak yer argument wi some force, Maister Meldrum. But I wad remind *ye* that we pursued a laddie called Frazer for just sic a crime a few months syne.

Meldrum: Ay, I ken that. He's noo lyin in the tolbooth. And makkin his penance in the toun's Kirks every Sabbath, dressed in sackcloth. Muckle tae the benefit o his immortal soul.

Stewart: Ay. But I'm still no shair ye understaun the practical difficulties.

Meldrum: I leave these tae ye, Sir James. I'm shair ye can find some wey tae pursue Tammas Aikenhead for this affront tae the Lord oor God.

Stewart: Maybe. Maybe.

Meldrum: And I'm shair that onie assize he micht hae tae thole will be just.

Stewart: We aye try tae assure *that*. But tell me meenister. This laddie has sair worried ye. Is he some kind o *rebel* or malignant d'ye think?

Meldrum: I've nae reason tae think it. He's anither kind o danger; an enthusiast for his cause. A zealot. And the Kirk is earnest in its fear o this... Deism. It's the kin o notion that appeals tae clever-like fowk. Especially young fowk.

Stewart: Like Aikenhead.

Meldrum: Just sae.

Stewart: Whit maks the Kirk fear this Deism as muckle as this?

Meldrum: (*after some reflection*) It's an *infection* o the body politic. An illness. A plague. And if it gangs unchecked it will spread till it finds its wey intae the very *vitals* o the Protestant faith. Intae the een and harns, bowels and heart... Everythin will be eaten awa wi doot, apostasy and atheism. And it'll no be God's Scotland, onie mair. But a reekin, blackened corse. Fit only for the maggots and worms that crawl in it...

Stewart: Ye paint a fearsome picture, meenister.

Meldrum: I paint the true picture, Sir. The picture o a land frae which God has withdrawn His grace. As he did frae the toon o Jerusalem.

Stewart: Jist sae.

Meldrum: And is Scotland onie dearer tae God nor Jerusalem was?

Stewart: I doot that.

Meldrum: As dae I. And then we'll be back tae the days o Charles the Second and his malignant brother...

Stewart: ...Swearin oaths tae the Bishops, and bein put ablo the boot and the thumbscrews if we dinna...

Meldrum: They were sair times for us aa, Sir James. The Lord be thankit they're gane.

Stewart: Amen tae that, meenister. Amen tae that. Sae! Tae extirpate this, ah, *infection* we maun mak somethin o an *example* o young Maister Aikenhead.

Meldrum: That wid be best. For the sake o the laddie's ain immortal soul's sake as muckle as for the souls o the fowk aroond him.

Stewart: As ye say. For the sake o his immortal soul. Very weel, Maister Meldrum. Let me think on the best wey to proceed.

Spence enters.

Spence: Advocate?

Stewart: Spence. Kindly show the meenister oot.

Stewart and Meldrum shake hands.

Stewart: Guid day tae ye, Maister Meldrum. Thank ye for bringin me yer information. I'll see whit I can dae wi it.

Meldrum: Guid day tae ye, Sir James. Thank ye for listenin tae me. May the guid Lord inform yer deliberations.

Stewart: (*smoothly*) That's aye my earnest prayer.

Meldrum leaves and Stewart resumes his seat.

Stewart: (*to himself*) I wonder... I wonder...

Spence returns.

Stewart: Spence. Wad ye rax me doon yon statute book. The yin frae last year.

Spence finds the book from the shelf and hands it to Stewart.

Stewart: Thank ye, thank ye.

He leafs through the pages, finds what he is looking for, and reads, muttering to himself as he does.

Stewart: Ay... I thocht sae... I thocht as muckle... Guid, guid...

He closes the book with a thud.

Stewart: Spence. I'd be maist obleiged if ye'd dae somethin for me.

Spence: Ay, Sir James?

Stewart: I'd like ye tae step oot intae the toon and ask aboot a laddie caa'd Tammas Aikenhead

Spence: A Tammas Aikenhead?

Stewart: Ay. He's a student at the toun's college. The meenister says he's a lood-moothit kin o chiel wha's been makkin a nuisance o himsel.

Spence: Ye tell me.

Stewart: I dae. Sae it shouldna be ower hard to find fowk wha ken him. Or ken aboot him. He's weel-kent amang the students, it seems. Ye micht stairt wi the college servants. That gaggle o bletherskites aye ken whit's goin on.

Spence: And whit kind o thing dae ye want me find oot aboot this mannie... Aikenhead?

Stewart: (*shrugging*) Oniethin. Everythin. As muckle as ye can. Just as muckle as ye can gaither.

Spence: Ay, Sir James.

Stewart: And efter ye've done that, wad ye oblige me further by steppin ower tae the Lord Chancellor's ludgins and askin his Lordship if he could spare me a few meenits o his day? There's a thing that he and I micht discuss.

Spence: Ay, Sir James.

Stewart: Oh, and afore ye gang. Another cup o warmed-up wine, there's a guid man. The year grows caulder by the minute.

Scene Four

The Lord Chancellor's chambers. Lord Polwarth, the Chancellor is taking his ease in a comfortable chair in front of a fire. There is a jug of wine on a small table beside him. Polwarth is a thin, clever-looking middle-aged man whose sardonic style conceals a hard-line Protestant politician. As Lord Chancellor of the Privy Council he is effectively the most powerful man in Scotland.

Stewart lumbers in supported by his faithful clerk, Thomas Spence. Polwarth waves him to a chair beside the fire.

Polwarth: I suppose I can interest ye in a gless o this?

Stewart: *(breathlessly)* On a day like this ye could *usually* interest me in a cup o het up piss. But naa thank ye. I've been soopin wine all mornin.

With some difficulty Stewart lowers himself into a chair opposite Polwarth. He dismisses Spence with a wave of the hand.

Polwarth: Suit yersel. The mair for me. But I'll drink tae yer health oniewey. Yer health, James.

Stewart: And yours, My Lord Polwarth. Damn yer title.

Polwarth: Still envious, James?

Stewart: I am that. But my day will come.

Polwarth: Of that I've *nae* doot.

He raises his glass again.

Polwarth: Here's tae yer advancement, my Lord Advocate.

Stewart: Noo *there's* a toast I'm aye happy tae drink.

The two men are plainly comfortable in one another's company, both at ease with power and influence. Stewart settles in the fireside chair opposite the Chancellor.

Polwarth: Dae ye ever miss the days in Holland when I was Doctor Wallace, and ye were...

Stewart: Plain Maister Graham. Naa, no ower muckle. Though hou ye got awa wi pretendin tae be a doctor I'll never ken.

Polwarth: A bottle o leeches and a shairp knife. Naethin simpler. Mair o a puzzle is hou *ye* managed tae pass as an honest merchant. Ye bein a lawyer and aa...

Stewart: Yer wit's no improvin wi age, Patrick.

Polwarth: Nor your wame, James. Look at the state o ye, man. Ye'll be deid afore the century's oot.

Stewart: *(shrugging massively)* Sae they tell me.

Polwarth: Weel, they tell ye richt.

Stewart: Whit's tae dae withoot makkin ma life intolerable. A man needs *some* comfort, and mine's the supper table.

Polwarth: And the bottle.

Stewart: The Guid Lord just didna see fit tae mak me a shilpit craitur like yersel, My Lord High Chancellor

Polwarth: Please yersel. But I'll miss ye when ye gang.

Stewart: Ay, weel. I'm no deid yet. Which is mair nor micht be said for that collection o walkin corses wha mak up His Majesty's Privy Cooncil in Scotland.

Polwarth: There ye micht be in the richt. There's times I rue the day they made me Lord Chancellor. Wheengin auld brutes.

Stewart: Yon's nae wey tae speak o yer fellow Privy Cooncillors.

Polwarth: I staund rebuked. Sae... whit can I dae for ye, My Lord Advocate?

Stewart: It's whit I can dae for *ye*, my Lord Chancellor.

Polwarth: Oh, I aye like a man wha says that. Are ye shair ye'll no hae some brandy wine. No lang aff the boat at Leith.

Stewart: Ach weel. Why not? But jist the smaaest measure.

> *Polwarth pours him a handsome measure which he sips appreciatively.*

Stewart: I've come, my Lord, tae deliver ye oot o the hands o the clergy. Tae relieve ye o the burden o the Kirk.

Polwarth: (*Laughs*) Aa these years, James, and I never kenned ye could wark miracles.

Stewart: I've jist had a visit frae the Reverend George Meldrum. Is he a man o your acquaintance?

Polwarth: The meenister at the Tron Kirk?

Stewart: *Ane* o the meenisters at the Tron Kirk, as he minded me. Ay, yon's the man

Polwarth: I ken o him. But he's no a man I'd gang oot my wey tae meet, tae tell ye the truth.

Stewart: Hou sae?

Polwarth: Ach I suppose it's auld history noo. But in '62 or '63 he buckled under tae the bishops at Aberdeen. He took the oath o obedience tae the Prelacy.

Stewart: Oh he did, did he?

Polwarth: Aye did he! I've seen the Privy Cooncil papers.

Stewart: Sae ye'd doot his judgement?

Polwarth: Wha kens? I'm disinclined tae trust onie man that's no married. Meenisters are queer-like fowk at the best o times. A single meenister, wi naebody in his bed but himsel and his God, maun be doubly odd.

Stewart: I'll mind ye I'm a single man masel.

Polwarth: Ay, but ye're no a meenister.

Stewart: May the Lord be thankit.

Polwarth: Indeed. But I'm telt that Meldrum's a guid eneuch clergyman. Whit wis the reverend gentleman callin on His Majesty's Advocate for?

Stewart: Tae inform.

Polwarth: Tae inform?

Stewart: Ay. He brocht me an interestin story. It seems that as he was leavin the Tron last nicht he was confrontit by a laddie caa'd Aikenhead, wha Maister Meldrum seems tae think is the deil incarnate. This young man, he says, has been spreidin the maist Godless blasphemy, atheism and *Deism* amang the students at the university...

Polwarth: ...And the meenister fears that if it's no checked, it will bring doon the haill Protestant policy aboot oor lugs. And alloo the prelates – tae whom he once swore his undyin allegiance – back intae Scotland. Was that it?

Stewart: Ay. That was it.

Polwarth: That's an auld sang, James. And hae ye no jist pursued some ither young man for muckle the same heinous crime?

Stewart: Ay. A prentis laddie caa'd John Frazer.

Polwarth: Which wis, if I mind aricht, recitin bits oot o some book or other?

Stewart: Blount's *Oracles Of Reason*. A maist seditious thing. And *De Veritate Religionis Christianae*...

Polwarth: By the Dutchman Grotius.

Stewart: The very man.

Polwarth: I've read that yin masel.

Stewart: Then shame on ye, ma Lord High Chancellor.

Polwarth: I'll just hae tae live wi my conscience.

Stewart: A gey uneasy livin companion, I wid hae thocht.

Polwarth: Sae. Maister Meldrum wants ye tae throw this young Maister Aitken...

Stewart: Aikenhead.

Polwarth: Young Maister Aikenhead intae the Tolbooth as weel. Where, I've nae doot, he wid hae a braw time exchangin notes wi Maister Frazer on their atheistical heroes. I dinna see muckle point in that.

Stewart: Nane at aa.

Polwarth: Sae?

Stewart: It's as plain as the neb on yer face that jylin James Frazer has done naethin tae deter the gab-moo'ed young atheists o the university.

Polwarth: Sae it wad seem.

Stewart: Sae instead o just *jylin* Maister Aikenhead, why no hing him.

There is a stunned silence.

Polwarth: Whit...?

Stewart: I *said*, instead o jylin Aikenhead we should hing him.

Polwarth: Hing him?

Stewart: That's richt.

Polwarth: Are ye gaun daft, man?

Stewart: I dinna think sae.

Polwarth: Ye maun be. Ye canna jist hing a body on the ward o a cack-brained meenister.

Stewart: Cack-brained he micht be. But there are hunners like him. And they're snappin at oor heels every time we step ower the door. Frettin and whinin at us tae dae somethin aboot aa the Godlessness and blasphemy that's gaen on.

Polwarth: True eneuch. But there's mair tae Scotland nor the Kirk.

Stewart: There's times I wonder.

Polwarth: Ay, I ken whit ye mean.

Stewart: Patrick. They want us tae tak this atheism and *Deism* seriously. Sae whit could be mair serious nor hingin somebody for it.

Polwarth: We canna hing somebody – even at the Kirk's behest – just like
  that. We need the law for it.

Stewart: We've got the law.

Polwarth: Whit law?

Stewart: Last year's act on blasphemy. The yin that the Security Committee
  – o which ye were a member – brocht in last year.

Polwarth: But that's nae guid. That's whit was used against young Frazer.
  And aa he's gettin is a few months in the Tolbooth and sair hurdies frae the
  repentance stools.

Stewart: Ye're gettin auld, Patrick. Ye're forgettin that last year's act ratified,
  approved and affirmed the Blasphemy Act o 1661.

Polwarth: 1661?

Stewart: And let me read ye whit the 1661 Act says.

  He extracts a document from his coat pocket and reads.

Stewart: "…His majesty, with the advice of the said estates, doth hereby
  statute and ordain that whoever hereafter, not being distracted in his wits,
  shall rail upon or curse God or any of the persons of the blessed Trinity,
  shall be processed before the Chief Justice, and being found guilty shall be
  punished with *death* …"

Polwarth: Even for a first offence?

Stewart: Even for a first offence.

Polwarth: Sae why wis it no used against young Frazer?

Stewart: Maybe it should hae been. It micht hae shut the Kirk up.

Polwarth: Naa, James. It'll no dae. The Majesty mentioned in the Act was
  Charles the Second. The very malignant that pit sae monie o us tae the horn
  – oorsels included – and declared us ootlaws. We canna use a tyrant's law
  tae hing a loose-tongued callant.

Stewart: The Kirk will love us for it.

Polwarth: Some o them micht.

Stewart: Maist o them will.

Polwarth: The worst o them will.

Stewart: It's the worst we want tae shut up.

Polwarth: Whit aboot the rest o Scotland.

Stewart: Let the Kirk tak care o the rest o Scotland. A blasphemer and an
  apostate is the next worst thing tae a warlock and a witch. And we've
  hingit – and burned – a wheen o *them* in the last few years.

Polwarth: That wis different.

Stewart: Ay. Maist o them were a lot mair innocent nor young Aikenhead.
  Rattle-pated auld wifies wha did nae hairm. Roasted tae keep the bigots
  happy. Can ye no see, man. We'd be usin the law o Scotland tae help
  uphold this Godly commonwealth o oors. Tae mak an example o a maist
  dangerous young apostate and blasphemer. Wha's poisoned wards are
  threatenin the immortal souls o some o the maist promisin young men in
  the capital city o this land.

Polwarth: Dae ye believe that?

Stewart: Whit difference does that mak?

Polwarth: I'm still no convinced. Throw him in the Tolbooth. Fine him till he squeals. But we canna hing him.

Stewart: Ay we can. The law is still on the statute book. The law says that blasphemers should be hingit. He blasphemed. Sae we hing him. Whit's wrang wi that?

Polwarth: Ye were aye a braw spieler, James Stewart. But a hingin…

Stewart: Look at the alternative. If we pursue him wi the ither end o the Act, as it were, aa we can mete oot is what we meted oot tae young Frazer. A spell in the Tolbooth and repentance in the Kirks.

Polwarth: It wid gie the whalp a nasty shock.

Stewart: It'll dae nae mair nor mak him a *hero* tae his philosophical admirers. I can see him noo. Sittin there in his sackcloth duds, smirkin. Bein railed at by some auld cuddie o a meenister – wha's got hauf his share o wit – while his smart friens frae the university snitter in the pews.

Polwarth: Ay…

Stewart: And we'd be laucht oot o every howff in Edinburgh.

Polwarth: I tak yer point.

Stewart: I'm tellin ye, Patrick. Hingin him is the richt thing tae dae.

Polwarth: Whit ye say maks sense. But I still dinna like it. There's shair tae be trouble. Frae the laddie's faimlie for ane thing.

Stewart: He hasna got a faimlie.

Polwarth: Aahhh…

Stewart: Mither and faither baith deid.

Polwarth: And whit kind o fowk were they?

Stewart: No whit ye'd caa stainless. His faither was hauled in front o the Privy Cooncil for peddlin love potions, wid ye believe? And his mither spent a month in the Tolbooth for stairtin a riot.

Polwarth: Mmmm. That maks a difference.

Stewart: Maks a difference? …He's perfect! A blasphemer oot o a nest o sinners. The Lord is deliverin him intae oor hands.

> *Polwarth lapses into silence. He is reflecting on the arguments. He is wavering – almost there but not quite convinced. Stewart decides to ram home his advantage.*

Stewart: And whit if the Kirk is richt? Hae ye thocht o that? What if this Deism *is* underminin the Protestant faith? What if it is aa aboot tae come tumblin doon aboot oor lugs? No the day. Mebbe no tomorrow. But some day…

Polwarth: It's a point. But no a very guid yin.

Stewart: Better nor ye micht think. Because the Stuarts and their bloody bishops are no ower lang hoot the door. And they're still sniffin aboot tryin tae get back in. And God help us if they ever succeed. I say, we need the guid will o the Kirk.

Polwarth: Save yer arguments for the assize, James Stewart. They micht frichten fifteen grocers and fishmongers, but they'll no wark wi me.

Stewart: Mebbe no. But it was only a few years syne that Graham o Claverhoos and his Papist friens were stravaigin aroon the hills. And chasin the King's airmy oot o the pass at Killiecrankie. A richt sair fleg that gied monie o us.

Polwarth: True eneuch.

Stewart: Wi canna risk oniethin, Patrick. No wi the Stuarts. Ye ken better nor me whit can happen tae a man wha falls foul o thae bastards. Dae ye want tae spend onie mair o yer days in some rank castle dungeon wi onlie the smell o yer ain shite for company?

Polwarth: I dae not. I'd raither glorify God in the Grassmercat.

Stewart: And ye'd no be the ainlie yin turned aff the hangman's ladder.

Polwarth: Ye'd be safe eneuch. Whaur wid they find a ladder – or a gallows – stout eneuch tae haud ye.

Stewart: (*ignoring him*) The point, Patrick, is that this laddie and his friends are roamin the land dingin it intae aabody's lugs that the Protestant religion – the very faith that underpins the state o Scotland – is naethin but a wheen o blethers. Some kind o daft-like fairie tale.

Polwarth: Ay… That does worry me.

Stewart: And sae it should. Especially when the French king's airmies are just waitin a chance tae pit the Papist Stuarts back on the throne. The very worst o the Papist Stuarts.

Polwarth: I fear ye're richt.

Stewart: O coorse I'm richt.

Polwarth: Ye mak a guid case, my Lord Advocate. There's nae doot aboot that.

> *Polwarth ponders for a while. Stewart looks on anxiously.*

Polwarth: Very weel. I'll support ye in yer pursuit o Maister Aikenhead.

Stewart: Guid! Ye'll no be sorry.

Polwarth: (*coldly*) If I am, James, I'll no be the only yin.

Stewart: And the Privy Cooncil?

Polwarth: There'll be nae trouble frae that quarter.

Stewart: Sae! We hing the young blasphemer.

Polwarth: No. We send the young blasphemer tae an assize.

Stewart: *Then* we hing him.

Polwarth: That, my Lord Advocate, depends on the assize.

Stewart: Ay, o coorse.

Polwarth: (*laughing and shaking his head*) Ye're a fearsome man, Stewart o Gutters. And that's no meant for a compliment.

Stewart: Jist an auld man daein his best tae keep the Scotland he loves on God's ain path. Here, gie me some mair o that brandy wine… aa this *persuadin* has gien me a terrible drouth.

> *Polwarth refills their glasses, Stewart raises his in a toast.*

Stewart: Here's confusion tae the King's enemies. And tae a successful prosecution. And, o coorse, tae the further advancement o His Majesty's Lord Chancellor.

Polwarth: (*with some irony*) God Save the King.

Scene Five

Meldrum is seated at his work table in his study. His full-bottomed wig is back on its stand beside his desk. He ruffles idly through the papers on his desk while he talks to the audience.

Meldrum: Sometimes I wonder at the Lord's wisdom in choosin the Scots as ane o His elect peoples. A mair ill-begotten collection o rank sinners and dirty delinquents never walked His earth. If they're no faain doon drunk they're at each other's throats or chasin each ither's wives, dochters and servant lassies. Maistly on the Sabbath.

He takes a piece of paper from his coat and brandishes it.

Meldrum: Nae surprise then, that the Kirk persuaded the Parliament o Scotland tae pass an act against...

He reads:

Meldrum: "drunkenness, Sabbath breaking, swearing, fornication, uncleanness and the mocking and reproaching of religion and the exercises thereof..."

He carefully folds the Act and inserts it back into the pocket of his coat

Meldrum: Sae, ye can see why young Maister Aikenhead chose his time badly. Naebody was in muckle o a mind tae listen tae his blethers aboot hou *unnecessary* their religion was. Or hou the Gospel o oor blessed Lord was naethin but the fancies in an auld wife's heid. Within a week o my ain visit wi Stewart o Gutters, oor young Deist had been served wi an indictment and thrown intae the auld Tollbooth...

Scene Six

The entrance-way to the grim old Tolbooth in the High Street of Edinburgh. Meldrum enters carrying a bundle. He is met by the turnkey of the Tolbooth.

Meldrum: Guid day tae ye, Sir.

Turnkey: Guid day meenister.

Meldrum: I've came tae see Maister Thomas Aikenhead.

Turnkey: *(indicating the bundle)* Is that for him?

Meldrum: It is.

Turnkey: I tak it there's nothin in there that will help the puir mannie escape frae oor hospitality?

Meldrum: Just ane or twa bits o food. And a religious book.

Turnkey: Ay weel.

> *They proceed to Aikenhead's cell. The youth is squatting on a heap of dirty straw looking decidedly the worse for wear. Meldrum retches slightly and covers his nose and mouth as he enters.*

Turnkey: A visitor for ye, Maister Aikenhead. Maister Meldrum o the Tron Kirk. I can see he's no muckle impressed by the odours that waft aboot yer ludgins. Sae ye're honoured by his visit.

Aikenhead: No the ward that wid hae occurred tae me.

Turnkey: Dinna be like yon, Maister Aikenhead. The meenister has brocht ye a puckle o gear tae while awa yer time. Ye'll hae to forgie him, Maister Meldrum. Aye an obstreperous faimlie, the Aikenheads. Did ye ken that his ain mither was wan o my guests a few years back?

Aikenhead: Mind yer tongue aboot ma mither.

Turnkey: Oh, a richt fearsome widow wumman wis that Helen Ramsay. It took three o the toon guard tae drag her in here. Whit was it she did?

Aikenhead: Mind yer ain business.

Turnkey: Oh ay. Broke intae an some apothecary's shop and caused a riot, as I mind it.

Aikenhead: The bastard owed my faither money. And widna pey it tae his widow efter he dee'd.

Turnkey: Oh ay, yer faither. Killed himsel by drinkin ane o his ain potions, did he? Ye see meenister, Maister Aikenhead's late faither was weel kent in Edinburgh as a man wha'd peddle certain *potions*. Certain potions that we're supposed tae – if ye'll forgie me Sir – help ye *perform* better. In certain weys. Wi weemin. If ye see whit I mean. Near poisoned a wumman yince and got hauled before the Privy Cooncil. Is that no richt, Maister Aikenhead?

Aikenhead: Awa an poke yer stick at some other caged brute, John Ritchie. This wan micht sink his teeth intae yer erse.

Meldrum: *(slipping the turnkey a few coins)* Thank ye, Maister Ritchie. I need tae hae a few wards wi Maister Aikenhead.

> *The turnkey leaves.*

Meldrum: I'm here tae let ye ken, Maister Aikenhead, that it was my information tae His Majesty's Advocate that led tae yer bein in this place.

Aikenhead stares at him thoughtfully, and shakes his head slowly.

Aikenhead: I thocht ye micht hae somethin tae dae wi it.

Meldrum: And I'd dae it again if I thocht it necessary.

Aikenhead: Nae doot. There's aye somebody in this toon ready tae drap a ward or twa intae the lug o ane o the law officers.

Meldrum: I can see that ye're aggrieved.

Aikenhead: Ye see richt.

Meldrum lays his small bundle in front of the youth.

Meldrum: I've brocht ye somethin.

Aikenhead: Whit?

Meldrum: Some cheese. Bread. Some oatcakes. A bit dried fish. A puckle wine. A book.

Aikenhead stares at the parcel and then at the minister.

Aikenhead: I'll no spurn yer gift. But I'll no thank ye either.

Meldrum: As ye please.

Aikenhead opens the bundle and begins to nibble at a piece of bread. He picks up the book, looks at the title, and tosses it into the straw.

Meldrum: Food for yer soul, Tammas.

Aikenhead: My soul, as ye call it, is my ain concern.

Meldrum: Yer soul is my concern. That's why ye're in this place.

The turnkey returns ushering Margaret Johnstone into the cell.

Turnkey: Another visitor for ye, Maister Aikenhead. Nae, ah, ongauns noo…

He exits. She looks bewildered and miserable. She runs to Aikenhead without a glance at Meldrum. They embrace. Then she notices Meldrum.

Margaret: Maister Meldrum…

She curtsies.

Meldrum: Guid day tae ye, Margaret.

Margaret: Hae ye come tae see my Tammas?

Meldrum: Ay lass.

Aikenhead: He's here wi food for baith my body and my soul. And tae confess.

Margaret: Confess?

Aikenhead: It was Maister Meldrum here that telt the Advocate aboot me.

Margaret: Telt? Hou de ye mean?

Aikenhead: It was the Shepherd o your flock that reported oor wee… conversation, tae His Majesty's Advocate.

Margaret: Conversation? Whit conversation?

Aikenhead: Ootside the Tron. A few nichts syne.

Margaret: That foolishness. Aboot Hell, and magicians and the like? Ye mean he *telt* on ye? Reported yer wards tae the King's officers?

Margaret is aghast.

Meldrum: For the sake o yer young man's soul, Margaret. That he micht repent o his wards, and gang nae further doon a maist dangerous road.

Margaret: Ye mean that my Tammas is in this... place... because ye took offence at that spiel o his on the steps o the Tron Kirk?

Meldrum: For the sake o his immortal soul, Margaret.

Margaret: May the Lord forgie ye, Sir.

Meldrum: I'm aye lukkin for the Lord's forgiveness, lass.

Margaret: But he's done naethin *wrang*...

Aikenhead: That's no whit the Advocate says, Margaret.

And he extracts a stained and crumpled copy of the indictment from his pocket and reads.

Aikenhead: The Advocate thinks I'm guilty o (*He reads*) "...horrid blasphemy, railing against and cursing our Lord and Saviour Jesus Christ, and impugning and denying the truth of the Holy Scriptures..."

Meldrum: Which I heard ye dae wi my ain lugs. And for which I beg ye tae ask the Lord's forgiveness.

Aikenhead: Forgiveness for what? For speculatin on the nature o the Lord's ain universe?

Meldrum: For the *manner* o that speculation.

Aikenhead: Ye mean for speculatin in a manner that ye and yer kind dinna approve o?

Meldrum: Tell me Tammas, de ye love this land o Scotland?

Aikenhead: (*taken aback*) Ay. I dae.

Meldrum: But ye wid raither it wis some kind o Papist tyranny? Like France? Or Spain?

Aikenhead: I wid not.

Meldrum: Then why dae ye want tae bring doon the wrath o the Lord oor God on this realm? Because that's whit ye are daein stravaigin aboot the land wi yer blasphemous utterances. Temptin his wrath. Invitin His punishment on us aa...?

Aikenhead: And is that your vision o God, Maister Meldrum? As a cantankerous auld man aye lukkin tae tak offence. Aye ready tae leather his bairns? He sounds worse nor my faither when he had a drink inside him.

Meldrum: It's whit the Guid Book tells us. And it maks yer blasphemy an offence against the realm. By provokin the maist powerful enemy o them aa – the Lord oor God.

Aikenhead: (*shaking his head*) Weel, meenister, I'm thankfu that I dinna share yer vision. Nor dae maist o my friens at the toun's college. Every nicht for the last three or four nichts they've gaithered below my window here tae cry my name. And gie me their support.

Meldrum: And ye find that a comfort?

Aikenhead: I'm no ower comforted. But I am encouraged. I'm encouraged tae think that I'm no the onlie yin in this Scotland that finds your holy scripture wantin.

Meldrum: I'm shair yer friens mean weel. But they micht be daein ye a grievous hairm.

Aikenhead: Hou sae? The mair that stand oot there and shout the better, I say.

Meldrum: Naa. The mair the worse. Can ye no see, laddie? That's *exactly* whit the Kirk and the State fear.

Aikenhead: Fear?

Meldrum: Ay, fear. That yer foolish ideas micht debauch and pervert His Majesty's Protestant subjects intae the error and superstition o this... Deism.

Aikenhead: It's no a superstition. It's a philosophy. As ye weel ken. But call it whit ye must.

Meldrum: Weel, whitever ye call it, the time has come tae repent o it.

Aikenhead: For the sake o my immortal soul, I suppose?

Meldrum: Ay! And for the sake o your *very* mortal neck. For God's sake laddie! I've seen that indictment against ye. And I've seen the list o witnesses against ye. D'ye no see the danger ye're in?

Aikenhead: Danger? For speakin whit I think?

Meldrum: The Advocate seems tae hae lined up some o yer friends and colleagues tae speak against ye. Includin Maister Mungo Craig.

Aikenhead: Ay. A fine irony that. Mungo Craig was the very man that *gied* me the books that led me tae Deism. And was the very man that was aye eggin me on tae speak oot. Noo he's tae testify against me.

Margaret: But I thocht Mungo was your frien?

Aikenhead: There are friens and friens, Margaret. But will fowk *believe* a witness like Mungo Craig.

Meldrum: They micht. They micht weel.

Margaret: Hoo lang will Tammas hae tae be in this place, Meenister? No for lang, shairly? No for just sayin a few things te yersel? It's no as if he's done oniethin *wrang*...

Meldrum: That depends, Margaret.

Margaret: On whit?

Meldrum: On the assize.

Margaret: The assize. He's tae gang tae an assize...?

Aikenhead: Dinna fret, Margaret. They canna dae ower muckle tae me. No for a thing like this. And no for a first faut, although I dinna see it as a faut masel...

Meldrum: I suggest ye read that indictment wi a bittie mair care, Maister Aikenhead. And the acts o parliament under which ye are bein pursued.

Aikenhead: Whit dae ye mean?

Meldrum: A nummer o things could happen tae ye. Ye micht just hae tae sit in the Tron Kirk for weeks on end, dressed in sackcloth whiles I preach at ye.

Aikenhead: Which is hou my, ah, fellow blasphemer James Frazer is repentin o his sins.

Meldrum: Ay. Or ye micht get fined a large pairt o yer incomins. Ye micht hae tae spend a wheen langer time in this place.

Margaret: Shairlie no...

Meldrum: Or ye micht also get *hingit!*

> *There is a gasp from Margaret and a stunned silence. The two young people clutch one another. When Aikenhead speaks his voice is cracking.*

Aikenhead: Hingit?

Meldrum: Ye maun ken that, shairlie?

Aikenhead: (*disbelieving*) Hingit! For a first faut?

Meldrum: Listen tae me, Tammas Aikenhead, and listen weel! The King's Advocate is no a man tae be trifled wi. If he wants ye hingit, and the assize agrees wi him, then ye'll be hingit.

Margaret: Oh no...

Meldrum: Then only the Lord – wha's very presence ye seem tae doot – can save ye.

> *The enormity of what Meldrum is saying, and the extent of his peril, seems to strike Aikenhead for the first time. He wilts, and his voice breaks.*

Aikenhead: Wid they dae that...?

Meldrum: Aye wid they!

Aikenhead: They canna! They canna dae that!

Meldrum: Ay they can.

Aikenhead: It wid be... the rankest cruelty.

Meldrum: That's no the wey they wid see it.

Margaret: It widna be allooed!

Meldrum: No allooed? Wha's tae stop them? The Kirk? The Kirk's no likely tae defend Maister Tammas Aikenhead, the famous Deist.

Aikenhead: The King...

Meldrum: The King? He spends maist o his time fechtin his war in Holland.

Aikenhead: Dear God... Whit can I dae?

Meldrum: If ye want tae save yer neck, young Sir, ye maun throw yersel on the mercy o the court.

Aikenhead: Hou dae I dae that?

Meldrum: Ye maun write a full – a very full – retraction o every Godless ward ye've ever uttered. And beg them tae desert the diet.

Aikenhead: (*in a show of feeble defiance*) I'll no gang on my belly.

Meldrum: Weel, ye can aye hing upricht.

Margaret: Tammas, listen tae Maister Meldrum. Listen tae whit he's tellin ye. Ye canna let them hing ye. No for some daft bit bletherin in the street.

Aikenhead: Ye're serious. Ye're no mockin me?

Meldrum: I'm no mockin.

Aikenhead: And If I write my... retraction... will that be the end o it?

Meldrum: It micht be. It micht no.

Margaret: They canna hing him, Meenister. No my Tammas. He's done naethin wrang. No really...

Meldrum: Let's hope no, Margaret.

Aikenhead: Will this petition serve? Will they listen?

Meldrum: There's no muckle else ye can dae. Unless ye're *determined* tae mak a martyr o yersel. For the cause o, eh, reason and Deism.

Aikenhead: Dear God. This canna be happenin.

Meldrum: It's happenin, Tammas.

Aikenhead: Whit should I dae?

Meldrum: A petition Tammas. Addressed tae the Lords o the Justiciar. But it'll hae tae be carefully written. And a strang and sincere admission o guilt and repentance.

Aikenhead: A petition?

Meldrum: Can yer Deistic conscience thole that, d'ye think? Because ye'll hae tae write things that micht stick in yer craw.

Aikenhead: Ye mean I'll hae tae deny every idea that I ever learned?

Meldrum: Are they ideas worth dancin on the end o a hangman's rope for?

Aikenhead: *(after some thought)* I'm no the stuff that martyrs are made o.

Meldrum: *(wryly)* No monie o us are, Tammas.

Margaret: Ye'll help him, Maister Meldrum. Tae write tae the court I mean.

Meldrum: If that's whit he wants. Is that whit ye want, Tammas?

Aikenhead: I suppose sae, ay.

Meldrum: Then I'll gie it some thocht this nicht and come back tomorrow forenoon wi pen and paper. Then we'll sit doon and draw up yer petition. I'll mak shair it gets tae the Lords o Justiciar, never fear.

Aikenhead: Thank ye.

Meldrum: But I warn ye, Tammas, onie sic petition will hae tae mak ye a man wha has seen the error o his Godless weys, and wants naethin mair nor tae lead a Christian life. Can ye accept that?

There is a silence.

Margaret: Tammas...

Aikenhead: Ay, I can accept that.

Meldrum: *(sardonically)* Ay, I thocht ye micht.

Aikenhead: *(with dignity)* Dinna mock me, Maister Meldrum. No when I'm in your hands.

Meldrum: Naa, Sir. We're all in the Lord's hands. But I accept yer rebuke. Ye hae my apology. Is it accepted?

Aikenhead: It is.

Meldrum: Then let the three o us pray tae the Lord our God that His mercy will prevail and that your petition will be accepted by the Lords o the High Court o Justiciar.

Aikenhead: *(with some fervour)* Amen tae that...

Scene Seven

Stewart's lodgings. Stewart is working at his table. Mungo Craig is ushered in. Stewart continues to write. Craig stands in front of him. Stewart ignores the young man. Mungo Craig coughs. Stewart still ignores him. There is a long and painful silence.

Craig: Ah… Sir James…

Stewart: (*not looking up*) Haud yer tongue Sir.

Craig shuffles awkwardly. Eventually Stewart looks up from the paper on which he has been scribbling.

Stewart: Ye are Maister Mungo Craig?

Craig: I am, Sir James.

Stewart: A student at the toun's college?

Craig: Ay Sir.

Stewart: And a frien o ane Tammas Aikenhead. Wha is noo lyin in the Tolbooth o Edinburgh?

Craig: No a frien. I widna say that.

Stewart: Then whit *wid* ye say?

Craig: An acquaintance, Sir. A fellow student. Mair that, I wid say…

Stewart: Ye tell me. Weel… I hae here a petition frae yer – fellow student – as ye call him, which claims that ye, Mungo Craig, were airt and pairt o the same wicked blasphemies wi which he is indicted.

Craig: (*indignantly*) That's never true, Sir. That's a wicked lie.

Stewart: Yer, ah, fellow student writes that the blasphemies he uttered were no his ain but were gotten oot o atheistical books. Books that he got frae ye, Maister Craig.

Craig: Ye canna believe that, Sir.

Stewart: That's whit he says. Spence, read Maister Craig here the appropriate bit o Maister Aikenhead's petition.

Spence: Ay, Sir James.

"…whatever expressions might have escaped me relating to any of the articles in the said indictment, the same was uttered or expressed by me, not as my own private sentiments and opinions, but were repeated by me as sentiments and opinions of some *atheistical writers* whose names I can particularly condescend upon, and whose books I did receive from *Mister Mungo Craig…*"

Stewart: Whose books I did receive frae Maister Mungo Craig.

Craig: This is the maist damnable injustice. It's no richt…

Spence: There's mair.

Stewart: Go on, Spence.

Spence: Maister Aikenhead gaes on tae describe Maister Craig as "…the chief and principal instrument who constantly made it his work to interrogate me anent my reading of the said atheistical principles and arguments therein contained…"

Stewart: The chief and principal instrument, eh?

Spence: That's whit Maister Aikenhead avers, Sir. His very wards.

Stewart: Sae. Accordin tae Maister Aikenhead...

Craig: A liar, Sir. A liar as weel as a blasphemer!

Stewart: ... Accordin tae Maister Aikenhead, not onlie did ye gie him the books oot o which he plucked his misbegotten notions, but ye encouraged him in them by... what were the wards again, Spence?

Spence: "... constantly made it his work to interrogate me anent my reading of the said atheistical principles and arguments..."

Stewart: Ay. By constantly interrogatin him on hou well he was gettin on wi his study o blasphemy. Whit were ye playin at, Maister Craig. Some kind o Deil's Catechism?

Craig: Sir. Nane o this is true, Sir.

Stewart: It seems tae me, Maister Craig, if whit he writes here is true, then ye should be joinin him in the Tolbooth, should ye no?

Craig: (*Now thoroughly frightened*) I beg ye, Sir. Dinna believe a ward o it. It's a haill pack o lies. The maist damnable lies.

Stewart: Maist o the fowk that stand where ye're standin tell me they're as innocent as lambs. Is that no the case, Spence?

Spence: It is indeed, Sir James.

Craig: But Sir. Ye canna believe what's written on that paper.

Stewart: And why no? Why should I believe whit ye tell me onie mair nor I believe whit yer 'acquaintance' Maister Aikenhead tells me? Just because ye're walkin aboot and he's no.

Craig: But Sir James...

Stewart: There's monie a rank villain walkin the streets o Edinburgh, Maister Craig. Ay and monie an innocent man has found his wey tae the Gallowlea in place o somebody else.

> *Craig is now thoroughly frightened and depressed. Stewart changes the mood.*

Stewart: Ay, it's a sorry business this, Maister Craig. A maist sorry business. Young men like yersel mixed up in aa this Godlessness.

Craig: Ay... Sir...

Stewart: Just hoo did a young man like yersel get involved wi this fellow Aikenhead? Eh?

Craig: It was at the college, Sir. We're in the same classes.

Stewart: Ye should hae picked yer friends wi mair care, should ye not?

Craig: Ay, Sir. I ken that noo.

Stewart: Ach weel. It's ower late for that. I fear that ye're hopelessly tarred wi the same brush as Maister Aikenhead. The same brush.

Craig: Naa, Sir. That canna be sae.

Stewart: I fear it is, Maister Craig. Yer acquaintance wi Aikenhead will be a sorrow tae ye in the years tae come.

Craig: That's no fair.

Stewart: Mebbe no. But the fowk o Edinburgh – at least the fowk that *maitter* – are a godly kind o fowk. They'll no be best disposed tae a man wha was a frien wi sic a rank and godless blasphemer.

Craig: No a frien, Sir. Haurdlie that!

Stewart: *We* ken that. But *they'll* no ken that. Ye'll aye be the laddie that was mixed up wi Aikenhead the blasphemer. I fear for yer prospects.

Craig: I damn the day I ever met Aikenhead.

Stewart: Yer evidence agin him at the trial will help, o coorse.

Craig: (*eagerly*) Ye think sae, Sir?

Stewart: Oh ay. But I doot it'll no be eneuch.

Craig: I wish I'd never clapped my een on the man.

Stewart: That's as micht be. There's no muckle ye can dae. Except maybe, somehow, put yer side o the case tae the guid fowk o Edinburgh.

Craig: My side o the case?

Stewart: (*sternly*) Maister Craig. Think on it. Ye've been painted as the deil in the whole affair. That's bound tae come oot at the assize.

Craig: But it's no true.

Stewart: That's as micht be. But the glaur will stick tae yer name, like shite tae yer shoe.

Craig: Whit can I dae?

Stewart: I dinna ken.

Craig: There maun be *somethin* I can dae...

Stewart: Weel. As I said – ye micht consider layin oot tae the fowk o Edinburgh the facts o the case. Your side o the argument, sae tae speak.

Craig: But hou wad I dae that?

Stewart: (*shrugging*) I'm no shair. Ye micht write somethin. A letter, perhaps or...

Craig: ...A pamphlet?

Stewart: A *pamphlet!* Noo that's a guid idea. A pamphlet. Whit dae ye say tae that notion, Spence?

Spence: It micht serve, Sir. It micht serve.

Craig: (*eagerly*) I could dae that. I could write a pamphlet.

Stewart: And if ye *dae* write yer pamphlet, I ken a bookseller wha micht be interested in publishin it.

Craig: That's richt guid o ye, Sir James.

Stewart: But hae ye ever written sic a pamphlet afore?

Craig: Eh... no Sir. I canna say that I hae.

Stewart: Weel, it's no as easy as it micht seem. There's a bit o skill tae it. A bit o an airt ye micht say.

Craig: I'd welcome onie advice ye micht like tae gie me, I'm shair.

Stewart: Hmmm... Weel, I'll tell ye whit. I've noted doon a few suggestions for ye. Just a few ideas. Ye micht want tae use them. Or no, as the case may be. It's up tae yersel...

He hands Craig a piece of paper.

Craig: Thank ye, Sir.

Stewart: As I said. It's up tae yersel whether or no ye use them. It's your pamphlet, no mine.

Craig: I understaun that, Sir. But I'm shair I'll find yer suggestions maist helpfu. Maist helpfu.

Stewart: Guid o ye tae say sae. And I got ane o my clergy friends tae suggest a few *appropriate* texts that ye micht consider incorporatin. It's aye a guid idea tae quote the Holy Scripture tae help advance yer argument. I suggest that ye consider them maist carefully.

Craig: Oh I will, I will. I canna tell ye hoo grateful I am for your coonsel and assistance.

Stewart: Tosh, Sir. It's naethin.

He laughs amiably.

Stewart: There was a while I thocht I micht hae tae invite ye tae share Maister Aikenhead's ludgins at the Auld Tolbooth. And mebbe his assize as weel...

He waves a hand, indicating that the interview is over.

Stewart: Spence will show ye oot.

Craig: O coorse, Sir. Thank ye Sir.

He offers his hand, but Stewart looks down at some papers ignoring him.

Stewart: Guid day tae ye, Maister Craig.

Craig: Guid day tae ye, Sir James.

As he turns to leave Stewart cackles behind his back.

Stewart: And guid luck wi the pamphlet. Mind an mak it interestin eneuch for fowk tae buy. Ye micht mak yersel a few bits o siller. And a young man like yersel can aye use some bits o siller, eh Maister Craig?

Craig exits to the sound of Stewart's laughter.

Scene Eight

Meldrum enters, dressed in his outdoor clothes. He carries a long walking stick.

Meldrum: Between us, Tammas an masel wrote a guid gangin petition. But their Lordships were haein nane o it. On November the tenth, he was hauled up tae a committee o the Privy Cooncil tae be telt that his petition had been turnt doon, and that he was tae gang tae an assize. And, whit's mair, their Lordships appointed Stewart o Gutters, the Lord Advocate himsel, tae prosecute the said process. The date was fixed for the 23rd o December – twa days before Oor Lord's birthday.

Sae! It's a gey frichtened young Deist that noo lies in the Edinburgh Tolbooth. Prayin heartily tae a saviour that he disna really believe in.

The turnkey enters, as cheerful and good-humoured as ever.

Turnkey: Guid day tae ye, meenister. Yer mannie's no himsel the day. Took his bit denner frae me withoot sae muckle as a curse.

Meldrum: Guid day tae ye, Sir. I doot we'll hae tae mak allowances for a young man that is sair frichtened.

Turnkey: Mebbe sae. But it's better for himsel that he keeps his strength and his spirits up.

Meldrum: That's true.

Turnkey: He'll need tae gie a guid accoont o himsel tae the assize. Naethin a Scots jury likes less nor a wan, shilpit craitur. I tell aa ma ludgers that.

Aikenhead is sitting disconsolate and alone in his pile of straw.

Turnkey: Here's yer man, meenister. I'll leave ye wi him. I've a busy day. There's an adulteress tae be whippit frae the Castle Hill tae the Netherbow, a beggar chiel tae be branded wi the toon's mairk, an a bairn-killer tae be hingit at the Gallowlea.

Aikenhead looks up sharply.

Turnkey: (*hastily*) An a wheen o fowk wha's debts hae been paid, and are tae be set free. They've aa tae be accoonted for in my record books. Sae I'll be scribblin and spellin maist o the day.

The turnkey leaves.

Meldrum: Guid day tae ye, Tammas.

The boy is silent.

Meldrum: This'll never dae, Tammas. Ye'll hae tae keep yer spirits up. That's the wey to gang afore the assize. Wi yer heid in the air. An honest Protestant, and loyal subject o His Majesty, wha's nae sweirt tae look onie man in the ee.

Aikenhead: Oor prayers tae the guid Lord tae persuade the court tae desert the assize didna dae muckle guid, did they?

Meldrum: Naa, they didna. And it's no for me tae say why. It's no gien tae onie man tae see intae the mind and purposes o Oor Lord. It micht be that he *wants* ye tae thole this assize.

Aikenhead: Maybe he wants tae hing me. As a punishment for readin Maister John Toland's book.

Meldrum: Oor Lord is merciful, Tammas.

Aikenhead: Is he?

Meldrum: Ay, he is.

Aikenhead: Ach weel. That'll be a comfort tae the man that they're aboot tae hing on the Gallowlea this very eftemuin.

Meldrum: The man killed a bairn.

Aikenhead: Then whaur was the Lord's mercy tae that bairn?

Meldrum: I doot ye maun see this, although ye'll no like it.

He hands Aikenhead a copy of Mungo Craig's pamphlet. The boy takes it, skims through it, starts to read.

Aikenhead: Dear God...

Meldrum: Ay, the man wishes ye ill. May the Lord forgie him for his enmity.

Aikenhead: The Lord micht. I'm no shair I can.

He reads:

Aikenhead: "A Satyr Against Atheistical Deism With The Genuine Character Of A Deist..." Good God... "To Which Is Prefixt An Account of Mr Aikenhead's Notions..." *(reading aloud in horror)* "... He pretends to be a great friend to reason which nevertheless he's acquainted with as an ass with mathematics... he would degrade Lucifer and lead the van of Hell himself... He's a mere ape mounted on the Pegasian wings of a rampant imagination..."

Meldrum: Ay. It's cruel. Cruel and unjust.

Aikenhead: And this is on sale, ye say?

Meldrum: I fear sae. At Maister Robert Hutchison's shop. At the head o the College Wynd.

Aikenhead: And is Maister Robert Hutchison sellin monie o them?

Meldrum: I believe he is.

Aikenhead: Dear God. *(he goes on reading)* Listen tae this. "He's a transcendental evil... a constellation fixed in direct opposition to all good... he's the excrement of the Creation, the ultimate butt of God's wrath, the subject of Satan's laughter and object of man's derision..."

Meldrum: Mebbe ye shouldna read onie mair, Tammas...

Aikenhead: That's *me* he's talkin aboot. A transcendental evil. But I'll tell ye somethin.

Meldrum: What?

Aikenhead: Mungo Craig never wrote this! "A constellation fixed in direct opposition to all good... the excrement of the Creation..." That's never Mungo Craig. Oh he's a clever eneuch chiel, but he's nae stylist. There's somebody else's hand here.

Meldrum: That micht be.

Aikenhead: But wha else hates me sae muckle?

Meldrum: I canna say that, Tammas.

Aikenhead continues to leaf through the pamphlet in horrified fascination.

Aikenhead: There's even a poem…

He paces the cell declaring in a bitter, mock-heroic fashion while Meldrum looks on helplessly.

"Come! let a rational and Holy flame,
Of zeal to Christ and God's most glorious name,
Our nation's honour, and our Christian right,
Inspire God's deputes with celestial light,
Who sit at justice; that they may atone,
With *blood* the affronts of heaven's offended throne…"

He stops and breaks down.

Aikenhead: (*through his tears*) Mungo, my man. Ye've done for me this time. Ye and yer booksellin frien Maister Robert Hutchison o the College Wynd. There's no an assize in Scotland will listen tae a ward I hae tae say. No efter this… thing!

Meldrum: Then we maun pray together that the Good Lord will fill the minds o the assize wi justice and their hearts wi compassion. Come Tammas. We'll pray thegither.

Aikenhead continues to stare at the pamphlet.

Aikenhead: "… that they may atone, with *blood* the affronts of heaven's offended throne." They want my blood, meenister. They want my blood.

Meldrum: Then let us pray tae the Lord tae deny them that blood. Will ye pray wi me, Tammas.

Aikenhead: (*shaking his head*) Pray wi ye? Whit for? It's plain tae me that yer God has set his face against me.

Meldrum: He's your God as weel as mine, Tammas.

Aikenhead: Is he? Are ye shair he's no Mungo Craig's God. The kind o God that alloos sic… *abominations* as this tae be selt on the streets o Edinburgh.

Meldrum: His weys are no tae be fathomed nor tested, Tammas.

Aikenhead: True. On the grounds that ye canna fathom or test that which disna exist.

Meldrum: I can understaun yer anger. But dinna let it drive the love o the guid Lord oot o yer heart.

Aikenhead: Love o the guid Lord!

Meldrum: Ay. Love. Because he loves ye nae matter whit ye micht think.

Aikenhead: Whit can I think? Syne the nicht I first clapped een on ye, Maister Meldrum, I've seen precious little sign o God's love. An ower muckle evidence o his spite.

Meldrum: Harsh wards, Tammas.

Aikenhead: There's mair if ye'd like. Dammit man, if ye'd just had the charity tae keep yer mooth shut I widna be in this stinkin place, bein *traduced* on the streets o Edinburgh by the likes o Mungo Craig. Wi my very life in jeopardy.

Meldrum: Ay ... weel ... I did whit I had tae dae.

Aikenhead: Ye didna hae tae gang runnin tae Stewart o Gutters. Naebody made ye. Except yer duty tae what ye call yer God.

Meldrum: I'll pray tae Him tae forgie ye for thae wards. They're spoken in anger and grief and fear. He'll understaun that they're no meant.

Meldrum raises his hands in the attitude of prayer.

Meldrum: Oh God. I ask ye tae forgive this thy servant Thomas Aikenhead, who, in this hour o great trial and anxiety, has spoken out against thy ineffable purpose.

Aikenhead: Ach, keep yer holy claptrap tae yer daft-like flock, ye auld ...

Meldrum continues to pray.

Meldrum: Grant him, O Lord, the strength tae bear the ordeal which his sins hae inflicted upon him, and the wisdom tae see the glory o thy weys. And give him, through the intervention o the sweet Lord Jesus Christ, the only Head and King o this Church, the peace that ravishes and passes all understanding. For thy name's sake, Amen.

While Meldrum is praying Aikenhead sinks to his knees and clasps his hands together.

Aikenhead: Oh Lord *his* God, I ask ye tae forgive yer humble servant the Reverend Clype and holy tell-tale George Meldrum, the meenister at the Tron Kirk in Edinburgh.

Meldrum: *(angrily)* Tammas...

Aikenhead: *(ignoring him)* Try tae mak him a better man, for the sake o aabody roon aboot him. I beg ye tae gie him mair sense o his ain worth, sae that he'll no hae tae gang greetin tae the King's Advocate for the revenge he miscries justice.

Meldrum: Haud yer tongue laddie.

Aikenhead: I'm near finished. Grant him, I beseech ye, the wit tae find his wey oot o this place and never tae return tae inflict his sanctimonious tosh on his poor victim, ane Thomas Aikenhead, aged twenty, viz masel.

Meldrum: This is a wicked blasphemy!

Aikenhead: And Lord, if they do hing me for castin aspersions on yersel, may the picture o my last dance on the Gallowlea haunt the Reverend Clype for the rest o his days. Day and nicht. Year in year oot. For *my ain* name's sake. Amen.

Meldrum is appalled at this display of bitter blasphemy.

Meldrum: The Lord My God will no be mocked. I can understaun yer anger and yer sorrow, but the Lord maun no be mocked. I'll leave ye tae regret yer bitterness. And pray that ye find it in yersel tae repent o yer blasphemous mockery.

Aikenhead: Ach, awa tae Hell wi ye.

Meldrum leaves.

Act II

Scene One

Meldrum is back at his work table in his study. He stares reflectively into space. His wig is on its stand beside the table. He addresses the audience.

Meldrum: Hae ye ever seen a good butcher at work? First he hings the carcase up, then wi ane lang cut spills the tripes oot ontae the flair. Then he carefully peels aff the skin, hacks aff the heid, then the limbs. Then efter he's reduced the beast tae its, eh, constituent pairts, he cuts them up intae bits and pieces smaa eneuch for fowk tae get their chops roond. Which is whit Stewart o Gutters did tae Tammas Aikenhead at that *travesty*, that reekin injustice they graced wi the name o an assize.

He stops, gets up, and begins to pace the stage with indications of mounting anger.

Meldrum: The laddie had nae chance. Aabody in Edinburgh kent that. Indeed, they had trouble assemblin an assize. Five o Edinburgh's mair decent fowk refused to serve, and were fined 100 merks each for their defiance. The fifteen men they did get were the kind o pious nonentities that are ower common in this toon. Ane o them was a *periwig* maker called Jerome Robertson. Which, I hae it on guid authority, is no his richt name. Wha in Scotland christens a bairn Jerome?

Ane efter the ither the witnesses – Maister Adam Mitchell, Maister John Neilsone, Maister Patrick Middletoune, Maister John Potter, and o coorse Maister Mungo Craig – were brocht intae the court. Tae swear on the Holy Bible that they had aften heard Tammas Aikenhead denounce the Holy Scriptures as sae much tosh and imaginins, and Christ himsel as nae mair nor a wily trickster. And, maist importantly, accordin tae Maister Mungo Craig, it was aa said in a scornin and jeerin manner – his very wards. A scornin and jeerin manner.

Meldrum resumes his seat at his paper-covered work table, but he continues to muse.

Meldrum: Puir Tammas! He did aathin he kent which wisna ower muckle. He begged, and he pleaded, he wept and he implored. He swore he wid never dae it or say it again. He renounced his atheistical books and ideas. He tried tae persuade them that since he was juist twenty and still a minor, he wisna fully responsible for his sayins. He thrashed aboot like a saumon on a gaff. It's a terrible sicht tae see a man seekin mercy when there's nane tae be had.

He breaks off and almost breaks down.

Meldrum: All fifteen men o the assize – includin Maister Jerome Robertson the periwig makker – were agreed. At noon on December the 24th they pronounced Tammas Aikenhead guilty o the crimes o cursin and railin our blessed Lord and scoffin at the Holy scriptures... After which the judges sentenced him tae be taken doon tae the Gallowlea and hingit. On the eighth day o January next tae come.

Through it all, Margaret Johnstone just sat there and sabbed, as her sweetheart squirmed and wriggled on the law's hook – the heuk that I had placed him on. The warst pairt for me was when Stewart caught my ee – and winked. He winked! His thocht wis clear. We'd done it thegither. Him and me. Stewart o Gutters and Meldrum o the Tron. The great Lord Advocate and the Reverend Clype.

Meldrum gets to his feet, and slowly begins to don his wig, overcoat and hat. He takes up his satchel and his walking cane.

Meldrum: Sae the next time I saw Tammas Aikenhead, it was in that awfae place whaur sae monie puir fowk hae gone tae confront their makker. The cell for the condemned in the auld Tolbooth o Edinburgh. The place they caa the Black Hert o Midlothian.

Scene Two

*When Meldrum is ushered into the Black Heart of Midlothian,
Aikenhead and Margaret are huddled together in the dirty straw. They
are trying to console one another. The turnkey is kindly.*

Turnkey: Anither visitor for ye, Maister Aikenhead. Yer guid frien Maister
Meldrum.

*Margaret turns her face away. Aikenhead regards him with a steady
gaze, then climbs to his feet and welcomes the minister with an
outstretched hand and a display of bitter mock-effusiveness.*

Aikenhead: Ah... meenister. Come in, come in. I'll no say mak yersel at
hame, because it's no the kind o place ye'd *want* tae be at hame in. There's
no even a proper chair for ye tae tak the wecht aff yer auld legs, just this
wee stool. But if ye'd care tae draw up some straw, I'm shair ye'll find it
maist comfortable. If ye dinna mind the smell that is... move ower
Margaret. Mak room for Maister Meldrum...

Margaret: Send him awa, Tammas. Whit dae we want wi him here? Him that
did this tae ye. Send him awa.

Meldrum: Tammas. I'm here tae...

Aikenhead: (*interrupting him*) Naa, naa, Margaret. The meenister has come
aa this wey. The very least I can dae is show him roon my new ludgins.
They're no ower big, I'll grant ye that, but they are historical. Oh ay, richt
historical.

Meldrum: Tammas...

Aikenhead: If I hadna read Maister Spinoza's correspondence wi Maister
Hugo Boxel on the subject, I'd even say it was croodit oot wi ghaists.
Ghaists o aa the fowk that hae sat in here waitin tae be... ah... introduced
tae their makker.

Meldrum: Ye can rest assured that the Haulie Ghaist is in this place as in
every place.

Aikenhead: Tae a convicted atheist such as masel, Sir, that is little
consolation. But it is no for naethin that they cry this place the Black Hert
o Midlothian.

Meldrum: Ay, a dark-like place richt eneuch.

Aikenhead: They also caa it the iron room, but in that they're wrang. It's no
iron. I've examined it all maist carefully. Nine feet wide, by nine feet wide
by nine feet high. It's made o guid heavy wuid. Oak, I wad say. But
strapped and *bound* wi iron. And maist firmly set in stane and mortar.

Meldrum: Tammas. I want tae speak wi ye. It's important that I speak wi ye.

Aikenhead: And the door that's just been banged ahint ye is inches thick.
Inches thick. Noo, the clever thing is... is when that door is shut, as it is
maist o the time, ye canna hear a thing. Nane o the screamin and shoutin
and fechtin and sweirin that's the usual music o the auld Tolbooth.

Margaret: It's a terrible place. And Tammas shouldnae be in it.

Meldrum: A formidable place.

Aikenhead: As ye say. But built wi great cunnin, tae mak a man despair.

Meldrum: Hou sae?

Aikenhead: D'ye no see meenister. There are nae distractions. Naethin atween a man and the thocht o his ain end. Naethin tae tak yer mind aff whit's ahead o ye. It's a place built – and weel built – tae mak ye despair.

Meldrum: Then fill yer mind wi the thocht o God's sweet love. Let Him that loves ye ravish ye wi his tenderness. Let His beauteous licht replace the darkness o yer despair.

Aikenhead: Hard tae dae, Maister Meldrum, for a man in my position.

Meldrum: Mebbe sae. But it wid drive oot the despair. And mak yer days on this earth mair eth tae thole.

Aikenhead: Sae ye tell me. But despair has a wey o creepin up on a man in a place like this. Every time I shut my een, there it is. Like a black, slaverin dug in the corner.

Margaret: Oh, Tammas...

Meldrum: Then let yersel fall intae the embrace o the Christ wha loves ye. There ye will find comfort. There yer soul will be redeemed. Otherwise ye are in great danger.

Aikenhead: I ken that.

Meldrum: I'm speakin o the danger tae yer very soul. Is it no written in the Gospel o Saint John that "...if ye believe not that I am He, ye shall die in yer sins..." Is that whit ye are seekin, Tammas Aikenhead. Tae die in yer sins...?

Aikenhead: Naa. I'm nae seekin that. I'm no seekin tae dee in or oot o sin.

Meldrum: But that will be yer fate unless ye repent o yer utterances. Unless ye mak yer peace wi yer God.

Aikenhead: Peace...?

Meldrum: Ay. And I've seen it wi my ain een. I've seen the peace that descended on the Godly men and women wha ascended tae glory frae the Grassmercat – no aa that lang syne.

Aikenhead: Ye mean the Covenanters?

Meldrum: I mean the Protestant martyrs of blessed memory.

Aikenhead: I saw ane o yer Godly men ascend tae glory. When I was only ten years auld. Renwick his name was.

Meldrum: Ye saw James Renwick hingit?

Aikenhead: Ma mither – a rumbunctious auld bitch but ane wi a pious cast tae her mind – wantit tae say a prayer for him as he passed on his wey tae glory. Sae she took me doon the Grassmercat, tae staund at the back o the crowd.

Meldrum: A terrible sicht for onie bairn.

Aikenhead: But bein the kind o bairn that I was, I wantit tae see whit was gaun on. Sae I gied her the slip, and wriggled ma wey doon through aa the fowk tae get tae the front.

Meldrum: The guid Lord preserve us aa. A bairn o ten years auld. Tae see sic a thing!

Aikenhead: Ay, it's no the kind o thing ye forget. And as I was gettin tae the front I heard Renwick's voice recitin a psalm. The ane hunner and third I think it was.

Meldrum: It was. (*reciting*) "... As for man, his days are as grass; as a flower of the field, so he flourisheth. For the wind passeth over it, and it is gone. And the place thereof shall know him no more..."

Aikenhead: The very wards. And bonnie wards they are. I got tae the front just as the hingman turned him aff the ladder. And d'ye ken whit I mind the maist clearly?

Meldrum: Terrible, maist terrible.

Aikenhead: Whit I mind as clear as oniethin, was the shite runnin doon his legs.

Meldrum: Ach...

Aikenhead: That's whit I mind. The shite rinnin doon his legs. And noo I canna hear that psalm, athoot the smell o shite in my nose and mooth. Then a man skelpit me roon the lug and telt me tae get the hell oot that place.

Margaret: Oh, Tammas... ye should pit sic things oot o yer heid. Ye shouldna sit here mindin on things like yon.

Meldrum: (*after a silence*) They were bad times for us all. There's nae doot aboot that. But James Renwick is noo in the airms o his Holy Faither wha loves and cherishes him.

Aikenhead: That's as may be. As for masel, meenister, I'd raither just *live*. For a while yet oniewcy.

Meldrum: Ay. Which is why I'm here tae see ye. Tae persuade ye tae go on arguin yer case.

Aikenhead: Argue my case? Wha's goin tae listen tae me noo. I argued my case at my assize, and precious little guid it did me.

Meldrum: Whit we maun dae is appeal tae King William.

Aikenhead: The King, ye say? In London? Or Holland? Or wherever he is maist o the time when he's fechtin his war against the French?

Meldrum: Ay. The King.

Aikenhead: Whit guid wid that dae?

Meldrum: Because he's promised aabody in this sufferin land o oors toleration. He micht be persuaded tae extend that toleration tae ye.

Aikenhead: Tae Papists, Quakers and prelatists ay. But tae a convicted blasphemer? A man whae has been condemned by an assize for cursin and railin at God?

Margaret: Wid he, d'ye think?

Meldrum: I dinna ken. But we maun try.

Margaret: Ay Tammas. He's richt. We maun try.

Aikenhead: (*shaking his head*) There's nae time. In five days' time they'll be pittin a rope roon ma neck on the Gallowlea.

Margaret: Tammas... dinna say sic things...

Aikenhead: It's true though. Five days. That's no eneuch time tae get messages tae London and back.

Meldrum: I've thocht o that. Whit we maun dae is petition the Privy Cooncil...

Aikenhead: *Anither* petition?

Meldrum: Ay. Petition the Privy Cooncil for a stay of execution. No for a pardon, but for a stay. If they'll grant ye that smaa mercy – and it is a smaa mercy – then we *can* get a message tae Kensington. I'll see tae that.

Margaret: Ay Tammas. It's worth tryin.

Aikenhead: Is it worth tryin? Mind whit happened tae the last petition.

Meldrum: It's that or sit here in yer straw until they come tae hing ye.

Aikenhead: Which is whit they want tae dae.

Margaret: But ye maun try, Tammas. Ye maun. Ye canna let them jist tak ye awa frae me. No withoot tryin. It's no richt. Ye've got tae try. Has he no, meenister? Tell him he's got tae try.

Meldrum: He's past bein telt by me, Margaret. And I canna say I blame him. But she's richt, Tammas. Ye maun try. For her sake as weel as yer ain.

Aikenhead: And for yours. Eh, meenister?

Meldrum: Ay. If ye like. For mine tae.

Aikenhead: I canna say that I feel ower obliged tae dae muckle for your sake.

Meldrum: For the sake o yer ain neck, then.

Aikenhead: That's an argument I can understaun just fine. Sae wha wid we address this yin tae.

Meldrum: Tae Polwarth.

Aikenhead: The Lord High Chancellor himsel.

Meldrum: And tae the rest o the Privy Cooncil. But Polwarth is the man we want tae get at.

Aikenhead: And is Polwarth and Stewart o Gutters no as thick as twa thieves?

Meldrum: They micht be. And he micht weel want tae see ye hingit. For reasons o his ain.

Margaret: Whit wey wid a great man like yon *want* tae hing my Tammas. I dinna understaun...

Meldrum: The weys o great men are mysterious, Margaret.

Aikenhead: Like the weys o the Lord.

Meldrum: But Polwarth canna ignore yer petition. And there are ither members o the cooncil wha'll mak shair o that.

Aikenhead: Sic like?

Meldrum: Auld Lord Anstruther. A maist kindly auld man. They say he's muckle agitated by yer case.

Aikenhead: Guid o his Lordship, I'm shair. Sae the same kind o petition as the last time?

Meldrum: Naa. Shorter. And this time ye write it yersel.

Aikenhead: And whit'll I say?

Meldrum: Accept the justice o yer sentence. Tell them ye were led astray by daft-like buiks. And tell them that ye are a convinced Christian man, wha wants nothin mair nor tae repent his wicked and foolish past.

Aikenhead: Crawl on my belly and lick their spittle? Again?

Meldrum: Ay. Again.

Aikenhead: Ach... Tae tell ye the truth meenister, I'm weary. I've been frichtened ower lang. There are times I feel that I canna wait for death tae come. Times I wish they wad come in that door richt noo and get it aa bye. And gie me some relief. Send me tae meet that God that ye keep tellin me aboot.

Margaret: *(fiercely)* Dinna ye talk like that Tammas Aikenhead. No in front o me. I'll no hae ye talkin like that. I want my ain man, and my ain hoose and my ain bairns. Like onie other wumman. I want your bairns. I'll no hae ye takin aa that awa frae me because ye're feelin wechtit doon wi... I just dinna ken whit...

The ferocity of her protestation startles him and puts some iron in his backbone.

Margaret: It wis this man that pit ye in this terrible place. And I dinna think I'll ever forgie him for it. But noo, mebbe he can help get ye oot. Ye've got tae try! I canna hae ye talkin like yon. I canna thole it. It's no... fair!

Aikenhead kisses the top of her head.

Aikenhead: I can see I've nae alternative.

Meldrum: Guid. I've brocht ye some writin materials. But afore we stairt, let us beg the Lord tae intercede. And let us demonstrate tae Him that ye are on His ain path. Tell me, were ye brocht up in the Kirk?

Aikenhead: Ay meenister.

Meldrum: And dae ye mind yer catechism, Tammas?

Aikenhead: *(hesitantly)* My catechism? Ay... I think sae. I think I can mind it.

Meldrum: Then I'll tak it. And yours, Margaret.

Meldrum takes a seat on a low stool, the only stool in the cell. The two young people stand in front of him. Margaret takes Aikenhead's hand. In soft voices they rehearse the Protestant catechism.

Meldrum: Margaret, what is the chief end of man?

Margaret: Man's chief end is to glorify God... and to enjoy him forever.

Meldrum: Tammas, what rule hath God given to direct us how we may glorify and enjoy him?

Aikenhead: The word of God, which is contained in the scriptures of the Old and New Testaments, is the only rule to direct us how we may glorify and enjoy him...

Meldrum: Margaret, what do the scriptures principally teach?

Margaret: The scriptures principally teach what man is to believe concerning God, and what duty God requires of man.

Meldrum: Tammas, what is God?

Aikenhead: God is a spirit, infinite, eternal, and unchangeable in his being, wisdom, power, holiness, justice, goodness and... truth...

The lights go down on the three figures.

Scene Three

Meldrum is ushered into the presence of Polwarth and Stewart. The Lord Chancellor at his business table, while Stewart is sitting, panting slightly, with a jug of wine beside him. Meldrum is waved to the side, into a chair before the table. There are no preliminaries. Polwarth is curt and businesslike.

Polwarth: I'm in receipt o Maister Aikenhead's supplication and I've taen the advice o Sir James.

Meldrum: And?

Polwarth: We're o a mind no tae grant it.

Meldrum: And micht I be permitted tae ask why not?

Polwarth: There's nae reason tae, Maister Meldrum. Or at least nane that either the Lord Advocate or masel can think o.

Meldrum: Is mercy no reason eneuch, gentlemen?

Stewart: Whaur's the mercy in drawin the haill sorry business oot. Better tae get it ower and done wi. That wid be merciful.

Meldrum: I doot that Maister Aikenhead wid see it that wey.

Polwarth: Forby, I'm no ower impressed by this petition o young Maister Aikenhead's. He says naethin here that he hisna said afore...

He reads it in an irritated manner.

Meldrum: He's no askin for a pardon. Just that ye prorogate the sentence for a while.

Stewart: But for hoo lang? A week? A month? A year? He disnae say hoo lang it'll tak him tae...

He peers across the table at the supplication.

Stewart: "... be yet reconciled to his offended God and Saviour".

Meldrum: Oniethin wid be better nor naethin. A week wid be better nor a day.

Stewart: Ay, and a lifetime better nor a year. But that's no exactly the point. The point is, why should we?

Meldrum: Then why should ye no? It wid be a smaa thing for gentlemen like yersel tae dae. It micht mean the difference atween God's redemption or Hell's fiery lake for Tammas Aikenhead.

Polwarth: I'll no bandy *theology* wi ye, meenister. But ye maun ken better nor us *why* the laws were passed under which Maister Aikenhead is noo condemned.

Meldrum is suddenly weary. He puts his face in his hands.

Meldrum: Gentlemen... please. I beg ye. This is no some wild, rantin, demagogue wha's oot tae stir up the Edinburgh mob. Oh he's persuasive eneuch, I grant ye that. And has a tongue on him that wid impress the Deil. But at heart he's just a confused laddie. An innocent.

Polwarth leans over the table and clasps his hands in front of him.

Polwarth: Can I tell ye a wee tale about innocents, meenister. When I was hidin oot frae Charles the Second in my ain faimly crypt, my dochter

Grizell used tae come oot at the deid o nicht wi a bit bread and cheese and somethin for me tae drink. But she had tae pass the Episcopalian curate's hoose, and yae nicht her passin waukent his dugs wha set up a fearful barkin and yelpin. Which, we thocht, micht lead the dragoons straucht tae me. D'ye ken whit happened?

Meldrum: I dinna, Sir.

Polwarth: The very next mornin my wife visited the curate and persuaded him that there was a spittle-chopped, lunatic dug loose in the neighbourhood. A mad yin! And for the sake o his wife and bairns he better *hing* his ain dugs.

Meldrum: And did he?

Polwarth: Aye did he! My wife is a fell persuasive woman. Sae, oot o love for me, and concern for *my* safety, my wife arranged tae hae three puir, dumb beasts hingit. Innocents wha'd done nae hairm tae oniebody.

Meldrum: I'm no shair I tak yer point, Sir.

Polwarth: My point, Sir, is that because o the love I hae for Scotland, I'm prepared tae let this whalp o a Delat a phrase ye've used yersel, I believe – hing. And I doot that he's as innocent as thae dugs were.

Meldrum: Tammas Aikenhead is nae dug, my Lord Chancellor. He's a man and possessed o an immortal soul. Which God cherishes.

Stewart: Then if God cherishes it that muckle he'll be gled tae tak it tae himsel. And wha's tae say a puir innocent dug hasna got a soul?

Meldrum: That's a blasphemy, Sir.

Stewart: Is it sae? Weel, if it is, I maist *humbly* beg yer pardon.

Meldrum: And yersel, Lord Polwarth? Are ye content tae see this young man hingit on the Gallowlea tomorrow efternoon?

Polwarth: I'm never *content* tae see a young man die, Maister Meldrum. But it was the decision o the assize. I've got tae abide by the decision o the assize. Whaur wid Scotland be if we didnae?

Meldrum: (*in a flash of irritation*) That assize was a mockery, Sir. Hou could it be otherwise efter that pamphlet o Maister Mungo Craig's. That was naethin but a demand for Aikenhead's bluid.

Polwarth: Maister Craig's literary efforts are no the business o His Majesty's Privy Cooncil, Maister Meldrum.

Meldrum: But what chance was there o a fair assize for the laddie efter *that*?

Stewart: (*harshly*) Hae a care, Sir. Like the Lord oor God, the courts o Scotland are no tae be mocked. Nor is the law tae be diverted.

Meldrum: My apology, Sir James. But he's no seekin tae divert the law. Aa he's seekin is a stay o execution. A few days o grace.

Stewart: Sae he says. But he's had since the twenty-fourth day o last month tae mak himsel ready for his eternal rest. If he's no ready noo, maybe he never will be.

Polwarth: It widna be there are *ither* plans afoot? Some kind o *petition* tae the King in London perhaps? Some appeal tae His Majesty's weel-kent sense o mercy?

Meldrum: He has a richt, shairly, tae dae whit he can tae save his life?

Meldrum and Aikenhead

Spence and Stewart

Polwarth: Oh ay. Naethin wrang wi that. He's just leavin it a bit late, that's aa.
The confrontation is beginning to anger Meldrum. He begins to lose
patience with Polwarth and Stewart.

Meldrum: Then if I canna appeal tae yer sense o mercy, gentlemen, let me
appeal tae yer sense o polity. There's a wheen o fowk oot there on the
streets o Edinburgh wha feel that ye're daein nae mair nor hingin a daft
laddie wha's just usin his bit book learnin tae shaw aff in front o the lassies.

Stewart: Is that what they say?

Meldrum: It is. They say that ye're usin the law tae kill a laddie wha's done
nae mair nor we've aa done in oor time. They dinna like whit they're seein.

Stewart: Dae they no?

Meldrum: Sae ye micht be faced wi a wee bit trouble frae the fowk o
Edinburgh tomorrow alang the road tae the Gallowlea.

Polwarth: James?

Stewart: (*shrugging*) There'll be a bit o unhappiness, ay. But a few dozen
fusiliers will mak shair it's nae mair nor that.

Meldrum: Ay. I dare say yer sodgers can haud the crowd back. But that'll no
stop the fowk o Edinburgh – as weel as the students and their teachers –
mutterin and murmurin against the cruelty o the Lord Chancellor and the
King's Advocate.

Polwarth: Are ye threatenin us, Maister Meldrum?

Meldrum: No, my Lord. Just anticipatin whit they micht say. That twa o His
Majesty's Privy Cooncillors widna gie a twenty-year-auld loon a few extra
days on this earth tae ready himsel for eternity.

Stewart: And I suppose that these mutterins and murmurins micht just find
their wey back tae His Majesty in London.

Meldrum: A man has a duty tae his conscience.

Stewart: As I mind it was your duty tae your conscience that brocht Maister
Aikenhead tae the gallows in the first place. Yer conscience seems tae be
an uncertain thing, Maister Meldrum.

Polwarth: As the Bishop o Aberdeen found oot mair nor thirty years syne.

Meldrum: (*taken aback by the reference to his shame*) Sir? Ye hae me at a
disadvantage.

Polwarth: (*smoothly*) When ye pledged yer allegiance tae Charles the Second
and his Bishops, Maister Meldrum. At the end o 1662, wis it no? That's
whit it says in the Privy Cooncil records.

Meldrum: (*breaking in*) That was lang syne, Sir. And it was different then...

Polwarth: Ay, it was different. But it was fowk like Sir James and masel
workin and hidin in exile that made it different. Workin and hidin in exile
tae deliver the Protestant Scotland we hae today.

Stewart: While other fowk – such as yersel – bided hame and took the
Bishops' oaths.

Meldrum: (*embarrassed and wrongfooted*) I find it hard tae see whit aa this
has tae dae wi Tammas Aikenhead. That's a different maitter entirely.

Stewart: The matter is hou muckle *wecht* we gie tae yer ward and yer
opinions meenister. First ye're ye're an avowed Presbyterian, then ye tak

the Bishop's oath, then ye're a Presbyterian again. Then ye come tae me tae tell me hou dangerous this Aikenhead is, demandin I dae somethin aboot it. Then when I dae, ye come beggin for his life.

Polwarth: Whit are we tae mak o aa that, Maister Meldrum.

Meldrum: *(trying to recover his composure)* I never thocht ye'd want tae hing him.

Stewart: Did ye no. Ah weel. We aa maun live and we aa maun learn. The Kirk and State baith agree that blasphemy is a *maist* serious offence. Punishable by death. That's the law. A man canna plead ignorance o the law. Especially an educated man like yersel.

Meldrum: But can ye no see the *cruelty* in whit ye're daein?

Polwarth: It's no me and Sir James that maks the law, Maister Meldrum. We just cairry it oot.

Meldrum: But where is the *justice* in hingin this laddie?

Stewart: There's aye a greater justice in upholdin the law o the land. Withoot it, then we hae naethin but chaos and darkness. Chaos and darkness.

Meldrum: My Lords, please. I'm no sayin that this laddie disnae deserve punishment. He does. But no hingit. No the Gallowlea. The laddie has the makkins o a guid Christian man.

Stewart: Weel, that's no my view o him. A mair determined young atheist I never heard. Despite aa his new protestations o piety.

At which point Meldrum realises he is defeated. There is a long silence.

Polwarth: Weel, Maister Meldrum. Ye've heard Sir James's views. And his are no far frae my ain. But I'm impressed by yer advocacy o Aikenhead's cause. And I'll no hae it said – especially frae the pulpit – that Patrick Hume o Polwarth, the Lord Chancellor o Scotland is an unfeelin or thochtless man.

Meldrum: *(with some irony)* I'm shair that naebody in the land wid think that.

Polwarth: Sae here's whit I'll dae. Tomorrow I'll caa a special meetin o His Majesty's Privy Cooncil and ask their Lordships tae decide whether or no Maister Aikenhead should hae a stay o execution. I can dae nae mair nor that.

Meldrum: Tomorrow?

Polwarth: Ay tomorrow. Ye widna expect me tae gaither up the auld brutes frae their various... ah... pleisures and diversions this eftemuin, noo wid ye?

Meldrum: I suppose not.

Polwarth: Very weel. Tomorrow it is. And I can promise ye this. There are eneuch tender-hearted members o the cooncil tae mak it a close run thing.

Stewart: And *I* can tell ye that baith Lord Fountainhall and Lord Anstruther hae been greetin in my lug aboot lettin young Aikenhead oot o the Tolbooth.

Meldrum: I'm richt pleased tae hear it.

Stewart: Ay, weel, it's no your lug.

Polwarth: The outcome o the vote will no be certain. Will that satisfy ye, Maister Meldrum?

Meldrum: No! I'll no be *satisfied* until I see the laddie oot frae the shadow o the Gallowlea. But I'll accept it.

Polwarth gets to his feet and extends his hand.

Polwarth: Guid o ye, Sir. Guid o ye.

Stewart: I'll no get up, meenister. I'm no the sprightly chap I used tae be.

As Meldrum turns and walks away, Polwarth calls after him.

Polwarth: Maister Meldrum. Seein I hae promised ye ane thing I'll promise ye anither.

Meldrum: Sir?

Polwarth: When the vote comes roon, I'll be for hingin him. The day eftir tomorrow.

Stewart smiles cheerfully. Meldrum leaves.

Stewart: Whit the Hell is Meldrum playin at?

Polwarth: Remorse mebbe? Ach, the man's a waiklin. He made that plain when he bent the knee tae the bishops.

Stewart: Ye'll never forgie him for that, will ye?

Polwarth: Should I? He's got nae stomach for whit has tae be done.

Stewart: But his frettin and complainin could mak trouble.

Polwarth: Then we'll just hae tae mak shair that the haill o Edinburgh kens that it was the Reverend Maister Meldrum wha informed on Maister Aikenhead in the first place.

Stewart: Which he'll then hae tae justify.

Polwarth: And mak himsel airt and pairt o the process which hingit the laddie.

Stewart: Guid. Guid. And nae protests oot o the General Assembly?

Polwarth: Not a bleat. Although I'm telt that Maister Meldrum is daein his best tae steir things up.

Stewart: But wi nae success?

Polwarth: Nane. The maist quiet and seemlie General Assembly for years. As quait as the grave.

Stewart: Or Peebles. My admiration for your... ah... skills kens nae bounds, my Lord Polwarth.

Polwarth: Guid o ye tae say sae, James. But they're exercised only in the King's interests.

Stewart: O coorse. Hae ye thocht Patrick, that perhaps it was God's ordinance that young Aikenhead should be hingit?

Polwarth: In that case, James, we're daein the Lord's work as weel as His Majesty's.

Stewart: (*slyly*) Micht it be, Chancellor, that the Lord's purposes and the King's are indivisible?

Polwarth: (*grinning*) Noo, where hae I heard that *blasphemous* thocht afore?

They laugh contentedly.

Scene Four

Meldrum, in his outdoor clothes, walks to the centre of the stage. He talks directly to the audience.

Meldrum: The Chancellor was as guid as his ward. When His Majesty's Privy Cooncil came tae vote, they were split richt doon the middle. Half o them wanted tae hing Aikenhead there and then. The ither half were for bidin their time. But the hail business was decided by ane man's castin vote – that o Patrick Hume o Polwarth, the Lord Chancellor o Scotland.

Margaret Johnstone enters. She is a disconsolate figure, wretched and red-eyed, her face puffed from weeping. She sees Meldrum and approaches him with one of her hands outstretched.

Margaret: I've come tae ye for money.

Meldrum: (*taken aback*) Money?

Margaret: Ay. I need money. Siller. For Tammas.

Meldrum: Whit wey does Tammas need money?

Margaret: Ye owe me, meenister. I need twa hunner merks.

Meldrum: Twa hunner… whit for wumman?

Margaret: My faither kens the Doomster.

Meldrum: The Doomster?

Margaret: Ay. The man that's tae hing Tammas.

Meldrum: But shairlie ye're no thinkin ye can pey him no tae… carry oot his duty?

Margaret: Wid tae God that I could. But he telt my faither that if I had twa hunner merks I could *pey* somebody tae pull on Tammas's legs. Tae cut short his strugglin.

Meldrum: Mercifu God!

Margaret: I've nae money. But ye hae. Ye maun hae money.

Meldrum: Dear God in Heaven.

Margaret: (*determined*) That's no a lot tae man like yersel. Twa hunner merks. Gie it tae me.

Meldrum: Margaret…

Margaret: That's aa. Just twa hunner merks. For Tammas's sake. If ye dinna gie me the money ma laddie could struggle a lang time on the end o the Doomster's rope.

Meldrum: Margaret. I canna gie ye money for ocht like that.

Margaret: Ye maun.

Meldrum: Naa, lass I canna. I canna pey to hae a man killed.

Margaret: (*almost puzzled*) But he's tae be killed oniewey. This is quicker.

Meldrum: It wad be wrang. It wad be a sin. I canna dae it.

Margaret: Hou can it be richt tae let him die slow, and be a sin tae kill him quickly. Oot o mercy.

Meldrum: Ye dinna unnerstaun…?

Margaret: (*impatiently*) No I dinna unnerstaun. And I dinna want tae hear. Just gie me the money.

Meldrum: I canna dae it.

Margaret: Ay ye can. Ye've got tae dae it.

Meldrum: I canna.

Margaret: Ye maun. Ye owe it. Tammas Aikenhead was aathin tae me. Ye stole him awa, wi yer clypin. Ye owe me meenister. Ye owe baith o us. Sae gie me the money, ye miserable auld...

Meldrum: Naa, wumman. I'll no dae it.

Margaret: Twa hunner merks. Please, Maister Meldrum. For pity's sake, please.

She sinks to her knees clinging to his legs.

Meldrum: No Margaret! No!

She gets up and stares at him contemptuously.

Margaret: Then I'll sell my erse in the Coogate.

Meldrum: Whit?

Margaret: There's just eneuch time left for me tae sell masel. If I can find eneuch men tae open their breeks. I'll gaither the money that wey.

Meldrum: In the name o God, Margaret.

Margaret: D'ye think I widna? Hou no? Am I no a bonnie eneuch quean? Is that whit ye think?

She hefts her breasts and flaunts her body seductively

Margaret: Are *these* no guid eneuch for onie man in Edinburgh? Eh meenister?

She turns her back on him, lifts her skirts and flaunts her backside.

Margaret: And is that no a bonnie sicht. There are plenty o men in this toon that'll pey me – and pey me weel – for a few minutes o that. Or tae tak their pintles in my mooth. Or tae sit my bare arse on their faces. Or tae let them pit their things up my...

Meldrum: Dear God lassie, dinna talk like this. This is the sheerest wickedness. This is the Deil himsel speakin through ye.

Margaret: The Deil is it? Then awa tae Hell wi ye. An I'll awa tae the Coogate tae mak use o the breists and hurdies that yer God gied tae me. If I canna keep them for Tammas Aikenhead, then onie man in Edinburgh can hae them. Sae long as he can pey. Includin yersel, meenister. If ye've a mind.

Meldrum: Damn ye wumman. I'll no be... *flaunted* at like this.

Margaret: Ach weel... the General Assembly's on just noo. There'll be ither *Godly* men wha are less *fasteedious* aboot whit they dae wi their wee bit pintles.

Meldrum: (*shouting*) For God's sake, Margaret. For the sake o yer immortal soul. For the sake o the laddie wha's tae dee tomorrow. Think o whit ye're daein...

Margaret: (*shouting*) Then gie me the bluidy money...

Meldrum fumbles desperately in the pockets of his greatcoat. He finds some money and thrusts it into her outstretched hands.

Meldrum: Here. Here. Tak it. Tak it. And may God hae mercy on baith oor souls.

Margaret: Sac lang as it buys some mercy for Tammas I'll no care whit happens tae ma soul. Or yours either. Especially yours.

> *She counts the money quickly.*

Margaret: It's no eneuch. Gie us mair.

> *He rummages again in his coat and thrusts more money into her outstretched hands. She turns on him with loathing in her voice.*

Margaret: Yer money micht pit an end tae his sufferin, meenister. But aye mind this. It was your miserable clypin tongue that killed him. It was ye that murdered a bricht laddie wha's backside ye're no fit tae wipe.

Meldrum: *(feebly)* The Lord our God will...

Margaret: Dinna talk tae me aboot yer *God*. No that bluidy monster. Ye'll no see me in yer Kirk again. I'll spit on the grund every time I pass its door. The Hell wi ye and yer God... And if ye want tae report me tae the King's Advocate, go ahead. I'll spit in *his* ee as weill.

> *With a final contemptuous shrug she rushes off leaving Meldrum aghast and drained. He buries his face in his hands for a long time.*

Meldrum: Dear God. Hoo monie mair sins can your servant's shoulders bear. Money oot my ain hand tae hae a man killed. And a guid, bonnie quean reduced tae *that*. That hissin, half-mad *serpent*. Filled wi poison and hate. Ready tae sell hersel on the streets, tae mak eneuch money tae brak the neck o the laddie she loves. Whit warlock's brew is this I've stirred. Show me Your noble *purpose* in aa this... *blasphemy?* Gie me some sign that Ye are *there*...

Scene Five

The Gallowlea on the road between Edinburgh and Leith. The Doomster (ie the public hangman) waits at the gallows. He cuts a strange figure, rather formally dressed in grey with silver trimming. He wears a beaver hat. There is the sound of a muffled drum.

Meldrum and Margaret enter. He is reciting psalm fifty-seven; she is sobbing.

Meldrum: "... Be merciful unto me O God, be merciful unto me: for my soul trusteth in thee; yea in the shadow of thy wings will I make my refuge, until these calamities be overpast...

Aikenhead enters, a Christ-like figure, unkempt, unshaven, wearing his 'grave clothes', ie the shroud. He is manacled but clutching a bible. He is escorted by two members of the city guard, dressed in red coats and carrying Lochaber axes.

Meldrum: "... I will cry unto God most high; unto God that performeth all things for me...

To the beat of the muffled drum, Aikenhead is escorted up the steps of the gallows, where he is met by the Doomster.

Meldrum: "... He shall send frae heaven and save me frae the reproach of him that would swallow me up. Selah. God shall send forth his mercy and his truth...

Aikenhead and the Doomster stand together on the gallows. Meldrum continues to recite, the Doomster waits patiently for the minister to finish declaiming.

Meldrum: "... My soul is among lions; and I lie even among them that are set on fire, even the sons of men whose teeth are spears and arrows, and their tongue a sharp sword... For thy mercy is great unto the heavens and thy truth unto the clouds. Be thou exalted, O God, above the heavens; let thy glory be above all the earth..."

The Doomster stares at the minister.

Doomster: Are ye feenisht, Sir?

Meldrum: (*nods*) For the present, Sir.

Doomster: Ay. Weel...

He reads aloud from a piece of paper.

Doomster: Thomas Aikenhead. It has been found proven by an assize that you are guilty of the crime of blasphemy; by cursing and railing our Blessed Lord, the second person of the Holy Trinity; by denying the incarnation of Our Saviour; by denying the Holy Trinity; by scoffing at the Holy Scriptures.

He pauses, and resumes his speech in a loud and sonorous voice.

Doomster: Therefore the Lords Justice Clerk and the Commissioners of the Justiciary have decerned and adjudged that ye be brocht here tae the Gallowlea, betwixt Edinburgh and Leith on this day, January the eighth in the year of Our Lord 1697, between the hours of two and four in the afternoon. There to be hingit on this gibbet till ye be deid, and your body tae be interred at the foot of this gallows. Which is pronounced for Doom.

Aikenhead listens to the pronouncement gravely and nods, as if approving.

Doomster: I maun ask ye Sir, hae ye a dyin declaration tae mak?

Aikenhead: (*in a throaty voice*) I hae, Sir!

Doomster: Then mak it.

Aikenhead steps to the front of the gallows. He begins his speech in a faltering voice.

Aikenhead: Christian people...

He stops, realises that his voice is too quiet to be heard and continues more purposefully, but reflectively.

Aikenhead: Good Christian people... It is a principal innate tae every man tae hae an *insatiable* inclination tae truth, and tae seek for it as his treasure. And *this*, I profess and declare, was the only cause that made me assert the things that I asserted, and deny the things that I denied... It was oot o pure love o truth that I acted. For I hae been ever, accordin to my capacity, searchin good and sufficient grounds whereon I micht safely build my faith...

He stops and reflects.

Aikenhead: Monie times hae I prayed as far as my *capacity* wad follow me. But I found always that the mair I thocht on God, the further I was frae Him. Frae my very heart, in grief and sorrow, I am perplexed and troubled for the base, wicked and *irreligious* expressions which I hae uttered. I did the same out o blind zeal to that which I thocht *truth.*

Meldrum: There is nae truth but God's truth!

Aikenhead: These things hae puzzled and vexed me. And all I hae learned is that I canna hae sic *certainty* as I wid hae. And sae, I desire aa men – especially ingenious *young men* – tae beware. And tak tent o thae things upon which I hae split...

Meldrum: Amen! Amen!

Aikenhead: (*harshly*) But I canna die athoot vindicating my innocence frae those abominable aspersions in a printed satyr o...

He spits out the name:

Aikenhead: *Maister Mungo Craig's*, wha wis a witness against me, and wha wis as deeply concerned in thae *Hellish* notions for which I am sentenced, as ever I was. Maister Craig will hae tae reckon wi God and his ain conscience. However, I forgie him and aa men. And wish the Lord tae forgie him likewise.

He hesitates and becomes more reflective again. Margaret's sobbing becomes louder.

Aikenhead: Like as I bless God, sae I die in the full persuasion o the true Christian Protestant Apostolic faith...

Margaret: Help him, God. Help him!

Aikenhead: Tae conclude. As the Lord in his providence hath been pleased in this exemplary manner tae punish my great sins, sae it is my earnest desire that my *blood*...

Margaret: Tammas...

Aikenhead: My blood may give a stop tae that ragin spirit o atheism which has taken sic a footin in Britain baith in practice and profession... And in his infinite mercy may he recover they wha are deluded wi these pernicious principles. Sae that His everlastin gospel may flourish in these lands, while sun and moon endureth...

He raises his manacled hands as if in benediction to his executioners.

Aikenhead: And noo, O Lord, Father, Son and Holy Ghaist. In thy hands I recommend my spirit, beggin and hopin for pardon tae aa my sins. And tae be received into thy eternal glory, through the only richteous merits o Jesus Christ my Saviour. To whom, with the Father and Blessed Spirit, my Sanctifier, be everlastin praise honour and glory. For noo and evermair. Amen...

He is hanged.

Margaret: (*Shrieking*) Tammas... Tammas...

Scene Six

Meldrum turns away from the hanging and walks to the front of the stage.

Meldrum: Sae that is hou they – or I should say *we* – hingit young Tammas Aikenhead. He died weel eneuch, wi proper contrition and praisin the Lord. That aye puzzled me. Tae this day it puzzles me. Was it Godly contrition? Was it an act o honest repentance by a man aboot tae meet his makker? Or was it somethin else? Some kind o devilish revenge on us, his persecutors? A stratagem tae leave us wi the notion that we'd hingit a blameless Christian?

Margaret Johnstone used the money I gied her tae hire twa strappin loons tae pull on Tammas's legs an brak his neck. Sae he found his wey tae eternity a few minutes faster nor he wid hae done – thanks tae the siller oot o my pooch. Puir Tammas. Puir Tammas.

He continues:

Meldrum: Oniewey... whit was left o him hung in chains on the gibbet for a few days tae be pecked at by the corbies. Then they took him doon and buried him on the Shrub Hill, just below the gallows. I've nae doot his spirit has joined the mournful band which is supposed tae flit across the Shrub Hill at nicht, girnin and wailin.

He laughs bitterly.

Meldrum: His, I venture, will be quotin passages frae Maister Toland and my Lord Herbert o Cherbury. As if the puir afflicted deid fowk didna hae eneuch tae thole...

He laughs again. Then he pauses and ponders.

Meldrum: The guid Lord, in his wisdom, seems tae prefer young men such as Maister Mungo Craig wha is noo flourishin as a man o business in Edinburgh. Mind ye, I did quite weel masel, becomin the Professor o Divinity at the toun's college, and Moderator o the General Assembly. Twice, nae less. The first time was in 1698, the year efter Aikenhead was hingit.

Sir James Stewart o Gutters is still His Majesty's Advocate, and can haurdlie walk across the High Street withoot his clerk tae haud him upricht. He damn near died in the year 1701, and noo tells fowk that it was my prayers that saved him. Which does naethin for my popularity in the toun. As for my Lord Polwarth... he is noo the Earl o Marchmont, and a very great man in the Kingdom. In the year of Our Lord 1702 was appointed His Majesty's Commissioner tae the General Assembly o the Kirk o Scotland. A fittin honour for a maist *pious* nobleman.

He stops and muses again.

Meldrum: But puir Margaret Johnstone didna fare sae weel. Her mither pit here oot o the hoose when it became plain that she was cairryin Tammas Aikenhead's bairn. And there was tae be nae joy in her bairnin time – the craitur was born deid. I found her wanderin aboot the Coogate amang the hoors and thieves, and took her intae my manse tae be my hoosekeeper. She was ower dispirited tae object. But it's an ill thing tae be looked efter by a young wumman that despises ye and disna ken hou tae hide it...

He removes his hat, coat and muffler and hangs them up. He ages visibly, seems to be paralysed down the left side, and shuffles painfully to a chair by the fire. He sits down and opens his bible on his knee. Then he calls out weakly.

Meldrum: Margaret...

Margaret enters, now aged almost thirty.

Meldrum: It's gey cauld... cauld...

She finds a shawl and drapes it over the old man's shoulders.

Margaret: It'll no be sae cauld whaur ye're gaen soon...

Meldrum: Whit's that ye say...?

Margaret: Ach naethin...

He dozes off. She looks down at him, not without pity. She ruffles what is left of his hair.

Margaret: (*shaking her head*) Puir auld deil... Puir auld deil...

She leaves. Meldrum is restive and mutters to himself.

Meldrum: A maist precious Kingdom... maist precious Kingdom... stretchin oot the boundaries thereof with blood... Maist worthy is the lamb that was slain... worthy is the lamb that was slain... worthy is the lamb that was slain... worthy is the lamb that was slain...

Aikenhead enters. The old man stirs from his reverie and opens his eyes. He is fearful.

Meldrum: Wha's there? Wha is it? Wha comes in ma hoose? Wha's there?

Aikenhead: (*gently*) Wheesht, meenister. Wheesht...

Meldrum: Tammas? Tammas Aikenhead? Is that ye?

Aikenhead: Ay, meenister.

Meldrum: I never thocht tae see ye again.

Aikenhead: I aye thocht tae see ye.

Meldrum: Did ye. Whit for?

Aikenhead makes no answer.

Meldrum: Is it my time? Is that it?

Aikenhead: Ay meenister. It's yer time.

Meldrum: Ach weel. I'm auld and done. I'm no sorry tae gang.

Aikenhead: That's as it should be.

Meldrum: But it wisna like that for yersel. The mair's the peety.

Aikenhead: I canna say it was. Are ye ready?

Meldrum: As ever I will be.

Aikenhead: Guid.

Meldrum: Will I be forgotten, Tammas? Will oniebody mind on George Meldrum o the Tron Kirk.

Aikenhead: There's aye somethin, meenister. A scrap o paper. An entry in a record. A note in somebody's accoonts. A name in a file. Twa wards on a heidstone. A thocht in somebody's mind. There's aye somethin.

Meldrum: But will they spit when they hear ma name? Will I aye be that wicked auld *clype?*

> *Aikenhead laughs gently.*

Aikenhead: Naa, meenister. But maybe as an ordinary man, wha did his best in sair and tryin times.

Meldrum: But wha's best wisna guid eneuch.

Aikenhead: Naebody's best ever is. We're aa the victims o oor ain days. Yersel as muckle as me.

Meldrum: Ay weel...

Aikenhead: Come awa wi ye noo, Sir. It's time tae gang.

> *Aikenhead helps the old man to his feet. Meldrum leans heavily on his arm.*

Meldrum: Hoo lang is it noo, Tammas?

Aikenhead: Hoo lang?

Meldrum: Since we last met.

Aikenhead: On the Gallowlea, ye mean? Oh... just ower twal year.

Meldrum: As lang as that. Twal year. My, my. I've never forgotten ye.

Aikenhead: I never thocht ye wid.

Meldrum: It's aye... troubled me. I've aye... fretted ower it.

Aikenhead: Ay. I ken.

> *Meldrum stops. He peers suspiciously at the young man.*

Meldrum: Ane question though.

Aikenhead: Whit?

Meldrum: That dyin declaration o yours.

Aikenhead: Whit aboot it?

Meldrum: Did ye mean it?

> *Aikenhead laughs delightedly.*

Aikenhead: Did I *mean* it? Oh dear, meenister. I can see we hae muckle tae talk aboot, ye and me.

> *They go off together.*